WHAT
HAPPENS
WHEN I DIE?

WHAT HAPPENS WHEN I DIE?

A Study of Life After Death

FaithQuestions SERIES

By George Hover

ABINGDON PRESS
NASHVILLE

WHAT HAPPENS WHEN I DIE?
A Study of Life After Death

Copyright © 2004 by Abingdon Press

This book is printed on acid-free, elemental chlorine-free paper.

ISBN: 0-687-04351-4

04 05 06 07 08 09 10 11 12 13—10 9 8 7 6 5 4 3 2 1

MANUFACTURED IN THE UNITED STATES OF AMERICA

CONTENTS

HOW TO USE
WHAT HAPPENS WHEN I DIE?
A STUDY OF LIFE AFTER DEATH

WHAT HAPPENS WHEN I DIE? provides opportunities to explore the research on a variety of life-after-death experiences and to compare them with the promise and hope of resurrection in the Christian faith. The book is designed for use in any of three settings. (1) adult Sunday school, (2) weekday adult groups, and (3) retreat settings. It can also provide a meaningful resource for private study and reflection. You will find foot notes and lists of words to use in Internet searches at the end of several of the chapters.

Sunday School: WHAT HAPPENS WHEN I DIE? may be used on Sunday mornings as a short-term, seven-week study. Sunday morning groups generally last 45 to 60 minutes. If your group would like to go into greater depth, you can divide the chapters and do the study for longer than seven weeks.

Weekday Study: If you use WHAT HAPPENS WHEN I DIE? in a weekday study, we recommend 90-minute sessions. Participants should prepare ahead by reading the chapter and choosing one activity for deeper reflection and study. A group leader may wish to assign these activities. You may also designate someone with computer skills to be your "webmaster." This person can search the words in "INTERNET KEY WORDS" and provide the group with additional information.

Retreat Study: You may wish to use WHAT HAPPENS WHEN I DIE? in a more intense study like a weekend retreat. Distribute the books at least two weeks in advance. Locate and provide additional media resources and reference materials, such as hymnbooks, Bibles, Bible dictionaries and commentaries, and books listed in the bibliography. If possible, have a computer with Internet capabilities on-site. Tell participants to read WHAT HAPPENS WHEN I DIE? before the retreat. Begin on Friday with an evening meal or refreshments followed by gathering time and worship. Do the activities in Chapter 1. Cover Chapters 2, 3, 4, 5, and 6 on Saturday. Develop a schedule that includes time for breaks, for meals, and for personal reflection of various topics in the sessions. Cover Chapter 7 on Sunday. End the retreat with closing worship on Sunday afternoon.

Leader/Learner Helps

Leader/learner helps are located in boxes near the relevant main text. They offer a variety of discussion and reflection activities. Include both the Gathering and Closing worship activities for each session, and choose from among the other leader/learner helps to fit the time frame you have chosen for your group.

The activities in the leader/learner helps meet the needs of a variety of personalities and ways of learning. They are designed to stimulate both solitary reflection and group discussion. An interactive and informal environment will foster a dynamic interchange of ideas and demonstrate the value of diverse perspectives. While the readings may be done in the group, reading outside of the session will enrich individual reflection and group discussion.

Most of the chapters include a list of further research options in the footnotes and in the lists of words in "INTERNET KEY WORDS." You will enrich your learning by reading one or more of the listed resources in the footnotes and by taking extra time for Internet research.

The Role of the Group Leader

A group leader facilitates gathering and closing worship, organizes the group for each session, monitors the use of time so that adequate attention is given to all major points of the session, and fosters an atmosphere of mutual respect and Christian caring. The leader should participate fully in the study as both learner and leader. The same person may lead all the sessions, or each session may have a different leader.

INTRODUCTION

When my son died, my world crashed. He was a leader, a writer, a powerful college football player; and he was killed instantly in a senseless accident. Not only did I feel a searing pain of loss and rage over my son's death, I felt it for the loss of dreams as well. I was disappointed that my Christian faith did not offer much consolation. It was hard for me to accept the teachings of Scripture on the basis of biblical authority alone. And there were so many questions. Is there really a life after death, or is this just wishful thinking? Will I see him again? If life can be so easily obliterated, what is life's meaning? If he is still living, where has he gone and what is he doing? Since he was not baptized, will that matter? What about Jesus' resurrection? Did it really happen? Can we expect a resurrection of our own? What about the peculiar events that happened after his death? What about psychics? Will people think I'm crazy if I talk about these things? How do I help my family deal with this grief?

This is my own story. As a pastor and professional counselor, I also heard other stories and other questions: My baby was stillborn. Will I see her in heaven? Will she always remain a baby?... My dad never made a decision of faith in Christ, and he did not live a very ethical life. What will become of him?... My daughter married a Muslim man, and the children are being raised Muslim. Will she be separated from them at death? Will they find salvation on another path?... My grandson talks about having lived another life, and gives details! Is this just his imagination?

All persons must deal with some of these questions at some time in their lives. For some Christians, the questions are answered in Scripture. The core of Christian faith is Jesus' resurrection and the promise of our own resurrection. Worship attendance on Easter Sunday, which celebrates the resurrection of Jesus, is one of the highest in the year. Fortunately, the resources of Christian faith are genuinely helpful for many who suffer the loss of loved ones.

Yet a profound experience of loss can undermine faith and spirituality. The devastation that follows the death of our loved ones, especially if they are children or spouses, is so great that some never recover; and others have their faith shattered. Mental health workers see people with cases of "frozen grief," whose lives or marriages seem to be stopped by an unresolved loss. Fortunately many of these people can be helped with good counseling. But even with the best of counseling, some survivors have grave difficulty in "letting go." I believe that letting go might be less difficult when survivors are aware of the vast research and evidence pointing to a life after death.

After the first agonizing weeks, and after they have begun to accept the reality of loss, people often begin to look for evidence concerning the fate of a deceased loved one. Some people, perhaps those with more scientific backgrounds, become desperate for resources to help them do their own investigation. They visit the library, bookstore, Internet, or even the movies, and discover a great deal of material. Some is useful; but many people have trouble finding resources that are thoughtful, authentic, and consistent with their Christian faith. Just as some people have little difficulty accepting the teachings of their faith about life after death, others have great difficulty. The general attitudes in our culture are quite materialistic, which has made it challenging for many, even Christians, to take spiritual reality seriously.

I searched fervently for answers to my questions. I began by reading Ring's work on near-death experiences, and Osis's work on deathbed visions (see Bibliography). Since these are scientific studies, they led to other resources on life after death. After about two years of research, I felt certain of Jesus' resurrection and of the likelihood of our own resurrection. I also had become convinced that the research supports the biblical record, and the biblical record supports the research findings. My local United Methodist church gave me the opportunity to present a six-session series. People appreciated the series. They said that the material was strongly faith-supporting and that it helped them become more certain that Jesus' resurrection extends also to us and our loved ones. I felt that I could help many people by offering these workshops, and at the same time, I could deal gradually with my own grief. I continue to present workshops in a variety of settings in different areas of the country.

This study book is a logical extension of the work I have been doing for about twenty years. I quickly recognized that this topic has wide public interest. People know how important it is to see the connections that exist between the human concerns about life, death, and resurrection and the scientific research on these topics. Church people are especially interested in the connections between these topics and the witness of the Scriptures. Examining the three areas together promises growth in both faith and understanding.

Biblical Views of Life After Death

One important issue is the mindset of the biblical writers in regard to life after death. While thousands of books have been written on this one topic itself, we try to reach the core by looking at some of the influences on the New Testament writers and the way that they used the Greek language to discuss their faith.

Most scholars agree that the Christian message involved a blending of the Pharisees' ideas about the Resurrection with Greek ideas about the immortality of the soul. This can be quite confusing. The Pharisees believed in the resurrection of the just, which would be something of a bodily resurrection. The Greek ideas were focused more on an "eternal soul" that transcends "the body." Several Greek words have meanings quite different from the modern dualistic view that we have simply a body and a soul. In Paul's use of these words, we see the blending of Hebrew and Greek ideas.

Sarx, usually translated "body" or "flesh," is used 147 times in the New Testament. It often suggests physical desires that become misguided and serve only the self, rather than others, or God.

Soma, usually translated "body," is used 142 times in the New Testament, usually indicating the body of human beings or animals, the body of plants, a body of people as a group. There is no suggestion of depravity. It refers to the physical structure that clothes the soul, an organizing principle that links flesh with life.

Psyche, usually translated "soul," is used 74 times and refers to the inner self, the principle of life by which a person exists as an individual. It includes mind and emotion.

Pneuma, usually translated "spirit," refers to the highest, nonphysical part of the self. It is used 291 times as "spirit," and 93 times as part of "Holy Spirit."

These four terms suggest a fourfold view of human nature, rather than a twofold view of mind and body; and such a view may be more sophisticated than modern views. Paul's writings have been central to the development of Christian faith, and in his clearest statement about the nature of resurrection, 1 Corinthians 15, he tells us that it is not the *sarx* that is raised, but the *soma*. Then Paul speaks of the soma that is physical and the soma that is spiritual. He does not say that the spiritual soma is saved and the physical soma destroyed. Rather, he tells us that the spiritual soma is resurrected as a gift of God, but in a soma different from the earthly soma. Similarly, modern research usually reports a "body" that is seen by the disciples, by the patient, or by those at the bedside. In Scripture, as well as in the research, some reports sound more visionary or "spiritual" and some sound more "physical," like the report of Jesus eating fish with the disciples after the Resurrection.

Some people discount reports of experiences that suggest life after death as fraud, hallucinations, wishful thinking, or reactions to drugs or brain changes. Yet discounting them is harder when we learn that there are literally thousands of such reports. Cautious researchers have found that many of these reports are NOT explainable as fraud, hallucination, wishful thinking, or drug reactions. Researchers have many unanswered questions, just as there are unanswered questions in studying the Old and New Testaments. The similarities between modern reports and the New Testament record are uncanny, and we will explore them in the course of this study.

The study of these issues, while not simple, creates in most students a new confidence in life after death and a new appreciation for the scriptural record concerning the resurrection of Jesus. One of the best ways for the churches to enhance their relevance to modern society is to explore and present Christian perspectives on these issues. This is the purpose of the following chapters.

Spiritually Transformative Experiences in the Bible

The Bible and the spiritual literature of other major world religions are filled with reports of mystical experiences of unity with God or the universe, bliss, visions, spiritual conversions, and illuminative experiences. If we narrow this very large field of research to reports most clearly touching on life after death in the Christian tradition, we can cite these passages, among many others, as related to our topic: the peace that passes understanding (Philippians 4:7; John 20:26), seeing a light (Matthew 4:16; John 1:4-5), seeing beautiful environments (Hebrews 12:22; Revelation 21:21), meeting people who are deceased, (1 Samuel 28:11-15;

Matthew 17:3; John 21:14), seeing angels (Luke 22:43), judgment (Hebrews 9:27; Matthew 12:36), forgiveness (Mark 3:28; Colossians 2:13), encounters with God (Genesis 12:7; Mark 12:26) or Jesus (Acts 9:5; 1 Thessalonians 4:17; Mark 16:12), out-of-body events (2 Corinthians 1:2-4; Ezekiel 1:24), a dynamic increase in love translated into social action (Amos 5:24; Matthew 5:43-44, 1 John 4:20, 2 John 1:5; 1 Timothy 6:11), and trust (Psalm 4:5; John 1:14; 2 Corinthians 3:4; 1 Timothy 4:10). In order to draw connections between the research findings concerning life after death and the witness of Scripture, we will look at near-death experiences, deathbed visions, out-of-body experiences, apparitions, reincarnation, and after-death communications. We will find that many of these reports touch on major themes in Scripture. We might say that the reports confirm the truth of Scripture, and the Scriptures confirm the truth of many of the reports.

A Note on Scientific Research

The issue of life after death is a profoundly important one. Naturally, in approaching this highly charged material, people will be influenced by their life experiences, which include education. For some, the scientific respectability of this approach to life-after-death studies will determine whether it is worth their time to pursue this curriculum.

First, we need to recognize that there are many valid models of scientific research. Good research always means keen observation and clear, open-minded thinking; but it does not always mean repeatability in a laboratory, as in some branches of research.

To give several examples: (1) Astronomers who study the birth and death of stars do not try to alter experimentally the behavior of the stars. (2) Pharmaceutical researchers who try to prove their drug works do not expect that 100 percent of patients will respond in the same way. (3) Few people would claim that a flipped coin cannot land standing on its edge, though many people have not seen this occur; and the great majority would not be likely to see it occur with repeated tries.

In short, the subject of the research influences the types of research that are possible. In studying life-after-death research, we are often dealing with events that are rare and that are experienced by particular people and described in the vocabulary of those people. In this area, several research forms are especially useful: (1) The case report, in which an event is described in ways that try to capture the particular nuances of the situation. (2) The observation of repeated patterns, as in reports of near-death experiences, deathbed visions reports, and out-of-body experience reports. (3) The experiment in the laboratory, as in Charles Tart's lab study of a purported out-of-body experience (see *Body Mind Spirit,* edited by Charles Tart; Hampton Roads Publishing Co.; 1997). (4) Meta-analysis, described by Gene Glass as the analysis of analyses—the statistical analysis of a large collection of analysis results, for the purpose of integrating the findings.

In laymen's terms, we believe that the evidence for life after the death of the body is very strong. Yet, because of the nature of the subject material, the kind of "proof" that is claimed in some areas of science may never be available on this issue.

As in the personal reports of the post-Resurrection appearances in the New Testament, we rely largely on personal reports of near-death experiences, deathbed visions, out-of body experiences, apparitions, reincarnation reports, and after-death communications. We find that many of these independent reports are nearly identical, cross-cultural, and recur over thousands of years.

Most of these personal reports are also independent of one another, and many events involved people who had never heard of the phenomenon they experienced. We believe that in most of these reports, there was no reason for people to fabricate and that most people tell the truth as they see it. In fact, there are probably more reasons for people NOT to report these phenomena, as in modern times they are sometimes subjected to ridicule, or in past times even death, as happened for some reporting the post-Resurrection appearances of Jesus. It is not reasonable to believe all of such reports are hallucinatory or fraudulent, any more than it is reasonable to believe they are all objectively true. Nor is it reasonable to believe that all modern laboratory and other reports are results of experimenter bias, in which experimenters see only what they wish to see. Further, the analysis of analyses in parapsychology shows the results are not due to chance, and these analyses are repeatable.

Finally, in recent years, there have been more than a few important scholars and scientists who have stated publicly that the evidence for life after death is strong and that serious research should be funded and pursued. Some of the larger Christian denominations and councils of churches should be contributing to this kind of research.

George Hover

CHAPTER 1
NEAR-DEATH EXPERIENCES

*"By their fruit you will recognize them. Not everyone who says to me
'Lord, Lord,' will enter the kingdom of heaven, but only he who does
the will of my Father who is in heaven."*

—Matthew 7:20-21, NIV

The near-death experience (NDE) has become a very lively issue. A visit to the bookstore or the Internet will show thousands of books, articles, and opinions that have been offered in the thirty years since the NDE has been systematically studied. In 1998, a consensus of near-death experience researchers and the Gallup Poll found that about thirteen million adults in the United States have had an NDE with at least some of the typical features.[1] This is 5 percent of the population. Opinions about the NDE vary greatly. Some Christians

> **Focus:** In this chapter we will explore the characteristics and effects of the near death experience (NDE), research on the NDE, and reflections on the NDE from a Christian perspective.

believe that the NDE is "of the devil" or a dangerous product of "The New Age Movement." Some focus on unpleasant or "hellish" experiences, but other Christian writers argue that the NDE may in some instances actually be a genuine encounter with Jesus or with God. Some argue that the NDE

Gathering

Keep in mind that the topic of life after death is profoundly important and goes to the heart of the New Testament message. It stirs deep emotions since nearly everyone has experienced or will experience the death of loved ones. Pray that this exploration will help deepen faith, that it will enhance understanding, and that those who have had recent losses will find comfort.

is a purely physiological reaction to brain disturbances or chemicals, and some point to NDEs that have happened to adherents of other world religions. For many the suggestion of life after death is the most attractive aspect of the NDE.

In light of this public interest, it is important for the church to explore the topic. Since the NDE has many implications for Christian faith, this chapter will approach the widely varying opinions from a simple but thoroughly biblical perspective, as indicated in the New Testament passage quoted above. We will look at the NDE in terms of its effects on those who have the experience. In order to do this we will examine and define the near-death experience, explore a sample of the research that has been done, and consider how the NDE may be understood from the point of view of Christian faith.

> What is your main interest is in studying this topic of life after death? What would you hope to have happen in these chapters? What do you know or believe about the NDE based on books, magazine articles, television, the Internet, your personal experience?

Frequency and Characteristics of the Near-Death Experience

Sometimes patients who have been resuscitated after an accident or surgery will report events that are quite striking. Medically speaking, these patients are comatose, or even brain inactive, but it appears that something quite mysterious is taking place.

As resuscitation techniques have improved over the years, the number of near-death experiences has increased. During the 1980's, researcher Kenneth Ring found that about 40 percent of the near-death patients he interviewed

> **Bible Study**
> Form teams of two or three. Review the characteristics of the NDE. Read the following Scriptures: Philippians 4:7; John 20:26; Matthew 4:16; John 1:4-5; Hebrews 12:22; Revelation 21:24; Luke 22:43; Hebrews 9:27; Matthew 12:35; Mark 3:28; Colossians 2:16; Genesis 12:7; Acts 9:5; 1 Thessalonians 4:17; Mark 16:12; Ezekiel 1:24; Amos 5:24; Matthew 5:43-44; 2 John 5; Psalm 4:5; 2 Corinthians 3:4. What does each Scripture suggest to you about life beyond death? about life prior to death? What characteristics of the near-death experience does the Scripture suggest to you?

reported one or more of about ten characteristics. These are now called "markers" for the NDE. Raymond Moody made a list of these markers, which includes (1) a sense of being dead, (2) peace and painlessness, (3) out-of-body experience, (4) going through a tunnel, (5) meeting people of light, (6) meeting a being of light, (7) a life review, (8) rising rapidly into the heavens, (9) a reluctance to return, (10) a different sense of time and space.[2] In the research, if a person reports one or more of these events, the experience is called an NDE. Many people have more than one component of the experience; very few have all the components.

Emotional descriptions sound much like spiritual encounters with God or Jesus, meetings with deceased relatives, heavenly visions, mystical or conversion experiences, or encounters with God's judgment. It is not uncommon for a person to describe the peacefulness in words like, "... if you took the thousand most beautiful things that ever happened to you and multiplied that by a million...."[3] Others describe a feeling of homecoming, a sense that the "real" self is separate from the body, or a light that is a light of love, "brilliant, but it doesn't hurt your eyes." Most people who have a near-death experience will say that they are completely convinced that there is life after death and that there is a God. They do not believe it, they know it, and they describe the NDE as the single, most profound spiritual experience of their lives. These reports remind us of the New Testament phrase, "the peace that passes understanding," and of passages that distinguish a spiritual body as different from a physical body, or some of the many passages where the writers refer to God or Jesus as Light.

Occasionally people describe frightening experiences. Maurice Rawlings, a cardiologist, has reported a number of such cases in *To Hell and Back: Life after Death—Startling New Evidence* (Thomas Nelson, 1996). He reports some of his patients being caught in a meaningless, bewildered existence, and seeing other "spirits" trapped by their own desires, hates, and fears. Such themes can be seen in Matthew 5:22-29 in which Jesus warned his listeners that they will be liable to judgment or the fires of hell if they remain angry or if they insult another. In Mark 9:43-48, he said that it would be better to lose a hand, foot, or eye and enter the kingdom of God maimed than

> Read Matthew 5:22-29; Mark 9:43-48; and Luke 12:15-21. What challenges you or makes you curious about each of these Scriptures? How do you think they relate to negative near-death experiences? positive near-death experiences?

17

Read the following Scriptures: Job 1:6-12; 2:1-7; Zechariah 3:1-2; Matthew 4:1-11; Luke 22:31-34; Acts 26:12-18; Romans 16:17-20; 2 Corinthians 2:5-11; 2 Thessalonians 2:9-12; Revelation 20:1-10. What is the role of Satan in these Scriptures? In view of the effects of the NDE on nearly all those who have them, what opinion can you form of the concern of some Christians that NDEs are the works of Satan? Do the frightening experiences reported by Rawlings undermine or confirm any validity to the NDE? Do you think the frightening experiences might be the effects of a guilty conscience? Why or why not? What do you make of the fact that reports of events like the NDE are more convincing to people who have had them than to people who have not?

to allow these body parts to cause a person to sin and to be thrown into the unquenchable fire where the "worm never dies." Luke 12:15-21 focuses on the hazards of making treasure a priority over a relationship with God.

Negative aspects of NDEs may suggest that people who align themselves with evil, destructiveness, hatred, or who refuse to shed arrogance or cynicism, may find their attitudes pursue them after death. However, most NDE researchers note that these negative experiences occur in only about 1 percent to 13.6 percent of NDEs, while the majority of NDEs are positive ones that express God's love and forgiveness.[4]

Children's Near-Death Experiences

For about thirty years, Melvin Morse, a pediatrician, has studied children's NDEs. Children's NDEs are especially impressive because children are less likely to be influenced by cultural and religious factors and probably have not read about the NDE. According to Morse, Kurt, aged 7, nearly died from muscular dystrophy compounded by pneumonia. After being without heartbeat for three minutes, Kurt was interviewed just hours after his resuscitation. " 'I saw Bonnie [one of the nurses present], and I said "hi" to her,' said Kurt. 'Then everything became dark, until I saw angels. I was in a beautiful place with flowers and rainbows, where everything was white like it had its own light. I talked to several people while I was there, including Jesus, who wanted me to stay with him. I wanted to stay there, but we decided I had to come back and see my parents again. I'm not afraid to go back to that place.' "[5]

Morse also tells about June, an 8-year-old girl who nearly drowned in a swimming pool when her hair became caught in a drain. Her heart had not been beating for the 45 minutes she received CPR. "All I remember was my hair getting stuck in the drain and then blacking out. The next thing I knew, I floated out of my body. I could see myself under the water but I wasn't afraid. All of a sudden I started going up a tunnel, and before I could think about it, I found myself in heaven. I know it was heaven because everything was bright and everyone was cheerful. A nice man asked me if I wanted to stay there. I thought about staying; I really did. But I said, 'I want to be back with my family.' Then I got to come back."[b]

Children may well be less influenced by cultural and religious factors than adults, but influence from parents can hardly be ruled out. Morse says that the characteristics of children in the years following their NDE are very striking. As young adults, they show a deep sense of purpose, a willingness to serve others, a spirituality far in advance of their years, a sense of being guided by God or by the Light, and a complete lack of the fear of death.

> How convincing are the children's NDEs to you personally? Does the fact that they occurred in children add to or subtract from their value? Explain your response. What do you think about the argument that children might have learned what to expect in the NDE at church, on TV, or from parents?

Validation Studies

Researchers have been creative in thinking of explanations for NDEs. Some assume the NDE is what it appears to be—a glimpse into another level of reality. Others say that patients who have NDEs are not "really dead." Raymond Moody observes that the legal definition of death in many states is the flat EEG and that a number of NDEs have occurred when the EEG was flat. Some consider NDEs to be hallucinations triggered by medical causes, psychological reactions to stress and fear, or changes in brain chemistry.

In the NDE research, Morse and others offer a number of studies that attempt to answer these questions. In one study, Morse found that of 121 children who were seriously ill but not near death, 118 had no experience at all to report, and the other three had dreams of white-coated monsters or the like. Another group of 37 children had been treated with a variety of medications, including anesthetic agents, narcotics, muscle relaxants, antipsychotics, antidepressants, and mood elevators. These children also had low oxygen levels, acid base disturbances, high carbon dioxide levels, and other combinations of problems. Morse reports that none of these children had any experience resembling an NDE.[7] If NDEs are caused or even partly caused by drugs, one would expect at least some of these children to have shown signs of NDEs.

In contrast to these two groups of children, Morse evaluated a group of 12 children who had survived cardiac arrest, of which 8 children reported visions of leaving their bodies and traveling to other places.[8] Morse strongly rules out drugs of all kinds as "explaining" NDEs and insists that the research shows there is only one known cause of NDEs—near death. For many years rather agnostic about the meaning of these NDEs, Morse now believes they are what they appear to be—glimpses into another level of reality. In the future, we will be receiving more definitive studies, based on larger samples.

Kenneth Ring in *Lessons from the Light* talks about another aspect of NDEs that is difficult to link to brain dysfunction or to drugs. Some patients, after their NDEs, report accurately on surgical procedures that took place while they were unconscious or on events in or outside the hospital about which they could have had no normal information.

> In view of the fact that some anesthetics, some illegal drugs, and in particular, ketamine, an anesthetic drug used especially with children, can trigger experiences that people report as "out-of-body," what do you think about the out-of-body component in the NDE?

A South African tells of his NDE. "While I was in a coma (and I believe clinically dead), my friend, the nurse, was killed in an automobile accident. I met her on the Other Side. She asked me to return,

> Make a list of the aspects of the NDE that are not explained by the arguments that NDEs are caused by medical or psychological or drug effects. Check your list against the following clues: accurate reports of conversations or events at the time the patient was supposed to be in coma, out-of-body reports of distant events, consistent pattern of NDEs, permanent impact on lifestyle of experiencers, blind people seeing when in the out-of-body state, conviction that there is a God and there is a life after the death of the physical body. What would you add to your list? What would you remove from your list?

promised that I would meet a loving wife, and asked that I tell her parents she loved them and was sorry she had wrecked her twenty-first birthday present (a red MGB). Needless to say, when I told the nursing staff upon my return that I knew Nurse van Wyk had been killed and the car she had been killed in was a red MGB (something only her parents knew) while I was 'dead,' people started to sit up and take notice."[9] If we assume that this report is true, what are we to make of the argument that NDEs can be explained by brain chemistry?

Long Term Effects of the Near-Death Experience

The NDE has profound long-term effects on patients who experience it. Interestingly, the effects also extend, in identical fashion but with slightly less magnitude, to those who merely hear about the experience. These effects are difficult to believe as stated, but are very well-documented. Kenneth Ring has done major work in this area and reports details in his book, *The Omega Project*. These long-term effects of the NDE include (1) an appreciation for life, extending to caring attention to small events of daily experience, (2) self-acceptance—feelings of inferiority give way to a sense of self-worth and confidence, (3) a concern for others translates into acts of compassion and an active desire to be of service, (4) a reverence for life that extends to concern for the environmental health of the planet, (5) anti-materialism and anti-

> List some other kinds of experiences people have that trigger the life changes and compare them to those of the people who have had near-death experiences as documented by Ring. First make the list, then look at clues: religious experience, a brush with death, a terminal illness, a drug experience, a sunset, a poem, a song, a Scripture passage, an interpersonal event? (There are others.) How permanent have you observed the changes to be?

Have a Debate

Position One: The NDE should be accepted for what it appears to be—a powerful and spiritually transformative event in which people sometimes have an encounter with God or Jesus.

Position Two: Until we know a great deal more about the NDE, it is better to explain it in "normal" or "scientific" ways (drugs, hallucination, brain changes).

competitiveness, (6) movement toward a wider, more inclusive spirituality, (7) a quest for knowledge and a sense of purpose, (8) a firm belief in God and a complete certainty about life after death.

The NDE in a Christian Context

The church has from the beginning believed that worship, preaching, the hearing of Scripture, the sacraments, and healing are channels through which the kingdom of God is most likely to penetrate our daily lives. Likewise, acts of charity and social involvement, dreams, and visionary or mystical experiences, have been held to offer glimpses of the kingdom of God. The near-death situation is another of those settings in which God may communicate most clearly. Several observations are at the heart of this belief. First, many who have near-death experiences report that it evokes both strong emotions and positive life changes. Second, many report encounters with God or Christ that leave them with a clear knowledge of God's loving judgment or God's loving forgiveness. Third, contrary to the influences of a materialistic culture, many emerge with a strong conviction of God's continuing presence with them and of life after death. Fourth, many view their own life after death as a gift from God and connect their experience with the resurrection of Jesus. Paul also made the connection

> What has been the effect on you of learning about the NDE? Does this change your feelings about your death and the deaths of loved ones? In what way? Explain.

when he wrote to the church at Corinth that Christ has been raised from death, as the guarantee that those who sleep in death will also be raised. (See 1 Corinthians 15:20-22.)

With the wide public interest in the near-death experience, it is important for the churches to address the many questions and concerns that are highlighted in NDE research. Pastors can help members of their congregations

> Form the group into two smaller groups. Members of Group One will imagine themselves as people who have had an NDE. Group Two members will imagine themselves as friends or pastors. Divide into pairs and have friends/pastors talk with NDEers about the experience. Report back to the larger group how your roleplay went.

by simply relating the nature and effects of the NDE. Kenneth Ring has described the NDE as a "benign virus" that should be spread around since its effect on hearers is nearly as positive as its effect on those who have the experience. Work with terminally ill patients has sometimes included showing the patient videos of people describing their near-death experiences. Depressed or suicidal patients have often been helped by studies of NDEs. Grieving people may be those most in need of this information.

Finally, a powerful effect of the NDE is that for most people, it permanently banishes the fear of death. This release often energizes those who experience it. It allows them to become less fearful, more responsible, and more compassionate. These changes are well-documented in the research on long-term effects of the NDE. This can amount to a conversion-like experience for those who have it. One person wrote: "I decided I had to tell what I had learned about this magnificent domain At the time, I had not heard of anyone who had gone beyond death. Millions upon millions feared death. Wouldn't they be glad to know that only the body dies, but not their inner person? I wanted to shout what I'd learned from the house tops, share it with all the people in the world."[10]

Closing Prayer

Consider the impact this chapter has had on you. Consider the desperation and sadness many people feel about death and their need to hear the message about eternal life. Pray that resurrection, which is the heart of the New Testament message, will happen increasingly in you, in your church, and in the world at large.

Notes

1. From "Life Beyond Death and Reincarnation," by Kent Davis Moberg, Spirituality Resource Center at *http://www.finalthoughts.com.*

2. From *The Light Beyond,* by Raymond Moody (Bantam, New York, 1988); pages 7–17.

3. From "Life After Death," by Kenneth Ring, Audiotape (Edgar Cayce Foundation, 1983).

4. From "Is There a Hell? Surprising Observations About the Near-Death Experience," by P. M. H. Atwater (Spring '92 *Journal of Near-Death Studies,* Vol. 10, No. 3).

5. From *Closer to the Light,* by Melvin Morse (Villard Books, New York, 1990); page 31.

6. From *Where God Lives,* by Melvin Morse and Paul Perry (New York: HarperCollins, 2000); pages 10–28.

7. From *Closer to the Light;* page 21.

8. From *Closer to the Light;* pages 21–23.

9. From *Lessons from the Light,* by Kenneth Ring, (Portsmouth, New Hampshire: Moment Point Press, 1998); page 64.

10. From *Lessons from the Light;* page 250.

For Additional Learning
Organize a Service Project
Find ways to discover if there are people in your group, your acquaintance, or in the congregation who have had an NDE. (There is almost always someone.) Ask them if they would be willing to share it with the group at some point. (This can also be profoundly helpful to the experiencer.) Some people will be eager to do so; some will be reluctant. Ask if anyone who has had an NDE would be willing to describe it on video so that it can be shown to terminally ill people or in educational settings. Then make the video available where needed.

Make a Drawing or Painting
Draw or paint something that conveys your view of the NDE or that represents a description by someone who has experienced an NDE.

Make a Life-After-Death Journal
In the journal enter Scripture passages, dreams, symbols, events, insights, conversations, newspaper and magazine articles, book excerpts, TV or movie program notes, poetry, music, or other things that relate to life after death.

For More Information
Internet Key Words—Type the following words and phrases into an Internet search program for additional information:

Near-Death Experience and Theology
Near-Death Experience and New Testament
Near-Death Experience Christian
Near-Death Experience
Near-Death Experience Research

CHAPTER 2
DEATHBED VISIONS

"What happens after death is so unspeakably glorious that our imagination and our feelings do not suffice to form even an approximate conception of it."

—C. G. Jung

"But filled with the Holy Spirit, he gazed into heaven and saw the glory of God and Jesus standing at the right hand of God. 'Look,' he said, 'I see the heavens opened and the Son of Man standing at the right hand of God!' "

—The Martyrdom of Stephen in Acts 7:55-56

An Overview

Deathbed visions (DBV) are first cousins of near-death experiences (NDE) and occur in patients who later actually die. Some dying patients encounter deceased loved ones and religious figures, report heavenly environments, and show surprising mood changes.[1] Studies show that only about 10 percent of dying patients are conscious at or just before death; but of those 10 percent, around 50 percent appear to have deathbed visions.[2] The DBV research illuminates several aspects of life after death more clearly than does the NDE research. These are (1) the frequent and detailed reports of meeting deceased loved ones or religious figures who arrive as heralds to a new dimension of life, (2) the lucidity of the patients, (3) the implications for

> **Focus:** This chapter will define and illustrate deathbed visions and their possible causes and explore them as evidence for life after death, as encouragement for interfaith understanding and as suggestions for relating to dying people.

> **Gathering**
> Pray the following prayer: "Spirit of God, give us a broader understanding of the complex issues in this research, an awe of the mystery of life and death, and a deeper compassion for the dying; in Christ we pray. Amen."
> Sing the hymn, "Arise, Shine Out, Your Light Has Come."

interfaith understanding, and (4) the suggestions for how we can relate to loved ones who are dying. DBV research also gives strong support to findings of other people who have studied the evidence suggesting life after death.

Jennie Is Here

This case was investigated by the British Society for Psychical Research, and very well documented. Two American children, Jennie and Edith, both eight years old, had caught diphtheria, and Jennie died. Edith was so sick that her parents decided not to tell her of the death of Jennie, her best friend. Before Edith died, she appeared to be seeing people who had predeceased her. Then, with surprise, "she turned to her father and said, 'Why Papa, I am going to take Jennie with me!... You did not tell me that Jennie was here!' And immediately she reached out her arms as if in welcome, and said, 'Oh, Jennie, I'm so glad you're here!' "[3]

> Form teams of two or three. Tell about a deathbed vision you have heard about or observed among your family or acquaintances. How have you interpreted it since it happened? How would you explain the striking DBV quoted in this section?

You Can Actually Do Research on Life After Death?

> If you were interested in whether DBVs are caused by drugs, brain changes, psychological, cultural, or religious factors, or rather by real visions of another level of existence, how would you set up a research project? What do you think of the statement that the researchers do not clearly describe how they chose the 877 reports that they followed-up? Do you see this as a problem? Why or why not?

In their book *At the Hour of Death,* researchers Karlis Osis and Erlendur Haraldsson describe a shrewd and ambitious project. They sent 5,704 questionnaires to medical professionals in India and the United States. In the questionnaires they asked about the medical professionals' observations of patients' deaths. One thousand seven hundred eight questionnaires were returned, and 877 were chosen for detailed follow-up, though the authors do not state how these latter reports were chosen.[4] The authors were primarily interested to see if DBVs support a confidence in life after death. As a result of the study, they do not believe they have proven life after death, but that the evidence from their research is quite convincing.

Causes of Deathbed Visions

Like the researchers on near-death experiences, Osis and Haraldsson were interested in the conventional arguments as to whether DBVs are caused by physical illness, drugs, hallucination, mental confusion, or psychological factors. They found that some of the patients did have these things occurring, but most DBV patients did not. Only 20 percent of the patients who had DBVs, for example, were receiving medication; yet all had some sort of vision or encounter or mood change.[5] Only a few of the Indian patients received any medication at all, yet the frequency of DBVs was no less than in U.S. patients.

An example is a vision that occurred in an eleven-year-old girl with a congenital heart malady. The caregivers were convinced that neither the drugs she was receiving nor her illness caused the vision. "She was having another bad episode with her heart, and said that she saw her mother in a pretty white dress and that her mother had one just like it for her [the patient]. She was very happy and smiling, told me to let her get up and go over there—her mother was ready to take her on a trip."[6] The child had never known her mother, who had died while giving birth to the patient. Osis and Haraldsson even suggest that, based on their study, medication inhibits rather than triggers DBVs.

> What do you think of the researchers' conclusions that drugs are most likely not involved in DBVs? If drugs were involved, would that make the visions less valid? Why or why not? How do you think that a patient can be lucid and at the same time appear to be communicating with a deceased person on another level of existence? How might we know that the patient did not suddenly lapse into hallucination?

DBVs and the Lucidity of Dying Patients

The researchers also found that patients who were most confused or incoherent were least likely to have DBVs. Patients who were most lucid were those who had DBVs. E. H. Clarke reported one of these cases: "Her mental functioning was perfect. She conversed, a few minutes before dying, as pleasantly and intelligently as ever. There was no delirium ... or ... symptoms indicating cerebral disturbance.... After saying a few words, she turned her head on her pillow as if to sleep, then unexpectedly turning it back, a glow, brilliant and beautiful ... came into her features; her eyes, opening, sparkled ... at the same moment, with a tone of emphatic surprise and delight, she pronounced the name of the [dead person] ... dearest to her; and then dropping her head upon her pillow ... [died]."[7] Mental confusion or hallucination do not seem to cause DBVs.

Does Fear or Expectation Cause DBVs?

Osis and Haraldsson also suspected that patients who were afraid of death might be more likely to have DBVs. It seems reasonable that, if patients feared death, they might "create" loved ones or religious figures in their DBVs. This did not happen. Some patients who expected to live would see visions of heavenly landscapes or deceased people and die, and some patients who expected to die would see visions of physical places, or living family members, and live. Patients also did not see in the visions people whom they had hoped would visit them in the hospital. In fact, the people seen in the visions, whether loved ones who had died before or religious figures, were most often unexpected and came with purposes of their own that surprised the patients.

> Form three teams to prepare the following skits:
> 1. One team member plays the role of a patient who is expected to recover and is having visions of beautiful heavenly landscapes. You are the bedside visitor. How do you respond?
> 2. One team member plays the role of a patient who is not expected to recover but has visions of earthly places and living people. How do you respond?
> 3. One team member plays the role of a patient who is lucid and suddenly appears to see someone who has already died, but the patient did not know about the death. How do you respond?

The case of Natalie Kalmus, one of the pioneer developers of the technicolor process, shows the complete surprise felt by the dying patient at the vision she saw. Kalmus was at the bedside of her dying sister, Eleanor.

"I sat on her bed and took her hand. It was on fire. Then Eleanor seemed to rise up in bed, almost to a sitting position. 'Natalie,' she said, 'there are so many of them. There's Fred and Ruth—what's she doing here?' An electric shock went through me. She had said Ruth! Ruth was her cousin, who had died suddenly the week before. But I knew that Eleanor had not been told of the sudden death.... I felt on the verge of some wonderful, almost frightening knowledge.... Her voice was surprisingly clear. 'It's so confusing. There are so many of them!' Suddenly her arms stretched out happily. 'I am going up,' she murmured."[8]

> What do you think about the idea that patients would create visions in order to reduce their fear? What do you think about the finding that many patients are surprised at whom they see in the visions? What do you think of the fact that patients did not see in their visions living people whom they had hoped would visit them in the hospital?

Do DBVs Reflect Religious Beliefs or Cultural Learning?

The researchers also wondered if DBVs were caused by religious beliefs, or if culture, age, education, and sex of the patients might be involved. They found that DBVs cut cleanly across all these factors. In Indian and U.S. patients, there were almost no differences related to age, sex, or education. Patients also did not indicate experiences that we might expect if the patients were strongly influenced by their religion or culture. U.S. patients did not report visions of hell, or judgment, or being whisked away by goblins or the grim reaper or the shadowy figures in the movie, *Ghost*. But they did meet deceased loved ones or Christ or God. Indian patients did not mention various levels or places in heaven, and there was little reference to karma or reincarnation or dissolving into God, all important teachings in Hinduism. Rather, they met deceased loved ones, Yama, or other Hindu deities associated with death, who usually came with a benign take-away purpose. Overall, the researchers believe that the similarities in Indian and U.S. DBVs were far greater than the differences. The differences seemed to lie in the way U.S. patients identified the religious figures as God or

> What conclusions do you make about the similarities of the DBV reports of Indian and U.S. patients?

Christ, while the Indian patients identified the figures as Yama or other Hindu personages associated with death. The DBV has a splendor of its own, apart from the influences of religion or culture.

Medically Unexplainable Mood Changes

Osis and Haraldsson also discovered that about 20 percent of patients showed a medically unexplainable elevation of mood shortly before death occurred.[9] The mood changes were almost always related to the recognition of loved ones or God and were expressed as ecstasy, relief, peace, and willingness to move on in the death process. A middle-aged businessman was dying and the healthcare person gave this report: "It was an experience of meeting someone whom he deeply loved. He smiled, reached up, and held out his hands. The expression on his face was one of joy. I asked him what he saw. He said his wife was standing right there and waiting for him.... He became very quiet and peaceful.... He was no longer afraid. He died a very peaceful death."[10] The researchers believe that this and many other cases they report suggest that the mood change is associated with the patients' encounter with another level of reality than with the medical factors we might expect.

Heavenly Landscapes, Earthly Landscapes

About 16 percent of both Indian and U.S. patients had visions of places or things.[11] These visions were of two types. In about two-thirds of the patients, the visions were of "heavenly" landscapes—gardens, gates, symbolic architecture. In one third of the patients, the visions were of earthly places or things.[12] Then the researchers discovered something quite striking: the patients who had "heavenly" visions were those who were *not* receiving medication known to trigger hallucinations. And the patients who had visions of earthly places were those patients who

> Consider: In a modern materialistic society, how can we take visions as reality? Do you think visions are just fantasy? Explain your response. How would we know if a vision is fantasy or not? What do you think about the notion that visions involve receiving signals from another reality or a deeper reality? How can we enhance our own ability to have visions? How does DBV research help or hinder answering these questions?

were given drugs known to trigger hallucinations. It appears that indeed hallucinogenic drugs trigger visions, but that visions of "heavenly" landscapes are not related to drugs. About 72 percent of patients report that the "heavenly" landscapes in their visions were places of great

> Look through the hymnal of your denomination and if possible some of the choral music. See how visionary experience is treated there. What images are in the hymns? What do these images say to you?

beauty.[13] Visions are at the heart of the issue of life after death, and most visions involve seeing, as in Isaiah's vision in Isaiah 6:1. But some visions seem to be mostly auditory, as in Paul's conversion on the road to Damascus in Acts 9:20.

What Can We Learn From DBVs?

Like NDEs, DBVs only rarely seem related to drugs, physical conditions, psychological reasons, age, sex, or educational achievement. And they are only slightly related to the patients' religious or cultural orientation. We also have learned that there is a consistency about the reports that we would not expect if they were caused by drugs, medical, psychological, cultural, or religious factors. Children's DBVs are similar to those of adults, and sometimes patients meet entities whom they did not know had died. NDEs and DBVs produce profound mood changes. Some agnostics and atheists report that although they did not previously believe in life after death, they have changed their minds after the NDE or DBV. All of these features, which challenge conventional explanations of the events, give serious support to a confidence in life after death and in a resurrection like Christ's, as promised in 1 Corinthians 15.

> Imagine that you are an atheist who has had an NDE or a DBV. What would it take for you to accept the experience or vision as evidence for life after death, as some atheist NDEers actually do. What do you think of the argument that the biblical ideas of soul, paradise, resurrection, peace, and communion with God arise from these kinds of visionary experiences? How do you think this research gives validity to these biblical ideas?

DBVs support Christian faith in other important ways. While deathbed visions are not mentioned directly in Scripture, the New Testament seems iridescent with its ideas about soul, paradise, resurrection, peace, and communion with God or Christ. Yet even with the influence of Christian ideas on Western culture, there is for patients a consistent element of surprise. DBVs appear to be events that happen to patients rather than being created by the patients. We suspect that ideas about soul, paradise, resurrection, peace, and communion with God arise from nonordinary human experiences, including DBVs, and are best seen as God's gifts to people in need. In their unexpectedness, they provide a vigorous argument for their validity. The idea that "visions" are genuine glimpses into another reality stretches our perceptions in the direction of authentic faith.

> Have you known of situations where bereaved people actually behaved as if they were confident that there is a continuing life, that God cares for their deceased loved ones, and that they most likely will meet again? Or have people you have known generally behaved as though they do not really believe in life after death? Tell about these situations.

If we reflect on the source of NDEs and DBVs, we see that spirituality is at its root experiential, based on powerful emotional events. Doctrine, theology, and intellect are important; yet the witness of the Bible is of people who are first emotionally influenced by their experiences. In this sense, NDEs and DBVs are not so different from the religious experiences that have been reported for millennia and documented in the sacred writings of various world religions.

Research on NDEs and DBVs leads us to another striking discovery: Jews, Christians, Hindus, Muslims, atheists, and nonreligious people have nearly similar experiences. DBVs of Christians and Hindus are almost identical except for the way the patient identifies the religious figure in the vision. These similarities suggest that all of us

> Consider your religious education. Was the focus on personal and emotional religious experience to an exclusion of doctrine and the use of memory for learning? vice versa? Or was there a good balance between learning about "visions" and about doctrine?

pass through the same gate at the hour of death. Since human beings have so much in common, NDEs and DBVs provide a point of common experience to help overcome some of the religious particularities that cause deep division in life. All humans are joined in living and in dying.

Many people need to believe that their worldview is more accurate than other worldviews, and strong psychological and social reasons undergird our commitment to our own way of seeing reality. One of the most important issues for people in the twenty-first century resides in a question: how do we develop sound emotional, intellectual, cultural, and religious foundations, and at the same time avoid the wars and persecutions that continually occur in the name of religion?

If ideas of the soul, resurrection, peace, paradise, and of encounters with God and with like-minded people who have died are universal in human experience, it is important that we respect all traditions and their ways of dealing with these universal human experiences. We may be fully committed to our own tradition, be willing to share our experience with believers of other faiths, and yet be receptive to learning from them as well.

Most world religions stress the centrality of love as the most important way to bridge the differences between people and societies. Love involves respect. DBVs have built into them this theme of love and respect that helps bridge even the chasm of the death of the physical body. One of the deepest meanings of life after death is that God

> What efforts are being made in your family, church, or community to enhance interfaith understanding? How could a presentation and discussion of this material on NDEs and DBVs contribute to deeper understanding?

loves and respects us both before and after the death of the physical body and does not limit us to this physical existence.

Melvin Morse, in his book *Transformed by the Light,* and Carla Wills-Brandon in her book, *One Last Hug Before I Go,* list ways in which the NDE and DBV can be helpful to patients and their families. For both patients and loved ones, these experiences lend control and dignity to the death experience. Spiritual visions help the patient interpret the experience of dying as a transition to another level of existence and a deeper connection with God and give a needed sense of connection with past generations. The visions help remove the fear of dying for patients as well as for visitors and medical personnel. Morse claims that 30 percent to 60 percent of American healthcare money is spent in the last few days of a patient's life. With a decreased fear of death on the part of medical pro-

> What have you observed about family visits to dying people? Have you had an experience of the extreme difficulty of these visits, and of not knowing what to say to the dying person? What did you do or say? Have you observed the mood of dying people to see whether they feel afraid and alone, or confident and supported by loved ones and by God?

fessionals and families, procedures that are costly might be avoided. The experiences can, if taken seriously, reverse the isolation and neglect of dying patients. And here is a striking discovery. It has been shown that family members who know about the DBV will spend more time at the sickbed. They can alleviate the isolation of the patient and the guilt of the family member who might otherwise have visited less frequently.

In terms of education, in the churches as well as in the culture in general, teaching people of all ages about NDEs and DBVs is one way to help students focus on experience and spirituality, in addition to material that emphasizes beliefs, doctrines, intellect, and memory.

Reports Can Be Beautiful, Moving, and Uncanny

Melvin Morse reports a DBV of an eleven-year-old boy with lym-

> Read Revelation 19:11-16: What challenges you or makes you curious about the vision reported by the dying boy? How do you think it inspires hope? Create a description of a deathbed vision based on what you have learned. Share with the group.

phoma: The boy said, "There are beautiful colors in the sky! There are beautiful colors and more beautiful colors. You could double jump up there! Double jump!" The next morning, opening his eyes wide, he asked his grieving parents to "... let me go. Don't be afraid.... I've seen God, angels and shepherds. I see the white horse."[14] The writer of the Book of Revelation, in 19:11 says, "I saw heaven standing open and there before me was a white horse, whose rider is called Faithful and True" (NIV).

Closing

Consider how the fear of death affects your life and the lives of your loved ones. Pray for God's guidance and strength to confront this fear. Express gratitude for the reports from dying people that encourage us to form loving and committed relationships and to trust that God cares for us at the time of death. Pray that those in need will gain a deeper understanding, a deeper Christian faith, and a sense of hope for the transition we call death.

Notes

1. From *At the Hour of Death*, by K. Osis and E. Haraldsson (Avon Books, New York, 1977); page 49.

2. From *Victor Zammit: A Lawyer Presents the Case for the Afterlife; Chapter 20. Deathbed Visions (www.victorzammit.com/book/chapter20.html);* page 2.

3. From *Psychical Research and the Resurrection,* by James Hyslop (Boston: Small, Maynard & Co., 1908), pages 88–89; quoted in *You Cannot Die,* by Ian Currie (Somerville House Publishing, 1998); page 182.

4. From *At the Hour of Death;* pages 49–50.

5. From *At the Hour of Death*; page 71.

6. From *At the Hour of Death*; page 67.

7. From *Visions, A Study of False Sight,* by E. H. Clarke, (Boston: Houghton, Osgood and Co., The Riverside Press, Cambridge, 1878), page 277; quoted in *You Cannot Die;* page 171.

8. From *You DO Take It With You,* by R. DeWitt Miller (New York: Citadel Press, 1955), page 193; quoted in *You Cannot Die*; pages 183–84.

9. From *At the Hour of Death;* page 120.

10. From *At the Hour of Death;* page 109.

11. From *At the Hour of Death;* page 161.

12. From *At the Hour of Death;* page 161.

13. From *At the Hour of Death;* page 169

14. From *One Last Hug Before I Go,* by Carla Wills-Brandon (Health Communications, Inc., Deerfield Beach, Florida); page 53.

For More Information
Internet Key Words—Type the following words and phrases into an Internet search program for additional information:

Deathbed Visions
Deathbed Visions Christian
Deathbed Visions Counseling
Deathbed Visions Hindu
Survival of Bodily Death

For Additional Learning
Arrange a Visit
   Contact a congregation of a different faith, and arrange for a visit and a dialogue. The goal should be to foster interfaith understanding, tolerance, and appreciation.

CHAPTER 3
OUT-OF-BODY EXPERIENCES

"I know a man in Christ who, fourteen years ago, had the experience of being caught up into the third Heaven. I don't know whether it was an actual physical experience, only God knows that. All I know is that this man was caught up into paradise. (I repeat, I do not know whether this was a physical happening or not, God alone knows.) This man heard words that cannot, and indeed must not, be put into human speech"
—2 Corinthians 12:2-4, JBP

A Number of Examples in Scripture

The Hebrew Scriptures and the New Testament report a number of events that modern people would call "out-of-body experiences" (OBE). Ezekiel describes one such occasion: "Then the Spirit lifted me up, and I heard behind me a loud rushing sound" (Ezekiel 3:12, NIV). Apparently this was not unusual for Ezekiel, since he also relates similar experiences in later chapters. The writer of the Song of Solomon describes an experience in chapter 5 that sounds like an OBE, but this one has to do with romance. In the Book of Revelation, John reports: "On the Lord's Day I was in the Spirit, and I heard behind me a loud voice like a trumpet" (Revelation 1:10, NIV).

Focus: This chapter explores biblical and contemporary out-of-body (OBE) reports, relates them to modern out-of-body experience research, shows how knowledge of the OBE is faith-supporting, and gives further basis for confidence in life after death and in spiritual discussions in a materialistic culture.

These reports sound alluring, confusing, strange, and exotic; but since the rise of modern science, the churches have not enjoyed much discus-

Gathering
Give thanks for the growing body of evidence that support a confidence in resurrection, both Christ's, and our own. Ask for strength to share the good news of the gospel with people who need to hear it.

sion of the out-of-body experience. Yet this is an important topic for churches to study. Not only are there the Scripture references, but there is increasing public curiosity about the OBE, thousands of reports by people who claim to have had OBEs, and a growing body of research literature.

Definition

The out-of-body experience is an event in which the location of consciousness is experienced by the subject to be outside of the physical body. In properly constructed surveys, in Charlottesville, Virginia, 25 percent of students surveyed and 14 percent of townspeople surveyed thought they had had an OBE. In Iceland, Erlendur Haraldsson found 8 percent that reported OBEs.[1] Like near-death experiences (NDEs) and deathbed visions (DBVs), these events are cross-cultural. While OBEs occur sometimes as one component of NDEs and DBVs, in this chapter we will focus on out-of-body events that happen to healthy people who are not in crisis and that sometimes are even voluntary. The OBE is widely thought to be one important source for ideas of the soul.

Bible Study

Read 2 Corinthians 12:2-4 from several different translations, including the King James Version. What do you make of the meaning of the differences in the way the passage is translated? Read Ezekiel 3:12 and Revelation 1:10. What thoughts do you have about the experiences described in Ezekiel, Second Corinthians, and Revelation? What other such reports are you aware of in the Bible? In your experience, how have church people interpreted such passages as these? What connections, if any, do you see between such passages and out-of-body experiences?

As with NDEs and DBVs, some researchers believe all OBEs are caused by physical or mental illness, drugs, brain changes or hallucinations, or are a special kind of dream. But it is not easy to explain all OBE cases in this way.

Four Types of Cases, Four Levels of Evidence

One writer on life-after-death-studies, Ian Currie, has suggested that there are four levels of evidence suggesting that the OBE is what it appears to be, an actual projection of a "spirit" from the physical body.[2]

Level 1: In these cases someone claims to have had an OBE but is alone during the experience and remains near to the physical body.

"Feeling tired, [Giuseppe] Costa threw himself on the bed without putting out the lamp on the night table. Accidentally knocking over the lamp as he turned in his sleep, he woke up to the smell of heavy smoke that was filling the room. Suddenly he found himself in the middle of the room, yet his physical body still lay on the bed, asleep. He now saw the room with much keener sight than with his physical eyes, 'as though a physical radiation penetrated the molecules of the objects.' He could see into the interior of his own body with 'its clusters of veins and nerves vibrating like a swarm of luminous living atoms.' He felt 'free, light, and ethereal.' When he tried to open the window of the smoke-filled room, however, he was unable to do so. He could see through the wall into the next room where his mother lay sleeping.... He watched her hurriedly get out of bed, run out of her room into the hall, and rush into his room and over to his bed, where she shook his physical body. At that moment he woke up with 'parched throat, throbbing temples, and difficult breathing.'"[3] Cases such as this are very convincing to the participant, but less so to others.

Level 2: These are cases in which the subject reports on events or situations that she or he was not in a physical position to see, but the reports are confirmed to be accurate by other people. We saw this kind of report in Chapter 1, in which the patient who is in a coma or near death later gives details of the surgery or of events in or outside the hospital that had occurred out of her or his physical sight during the operation or during clinical death. These events are eerie and difficult for some people to believe. There are hundreds of such cases. The subject, and often those who only hear of the event, become convinced of a life after death.

Level 3: In these cases the individual projects herself or himself to a place distant from the physical body and is seen in apparitional form by other people present. These cases happen less frequently than those on Levels 1 and 2, but some are very well documented and researched.

An English clergyman, W. T. Stead, presented this case. A member of his church was at home with a fever during an evening service. As the service progressed, the woman (or her double) walked down the aisle in view of the congregation, sat in an empty pew, picked up a hymn book but did not sing and did not contribute to the collection when the plate was passed. At the end of the service, she stood up, walked quickly up the aisle, opened the door, and left. According to Stead, she had recently joined the church, and sat in the pew she normally occupied. Later, Stead learned that she had wanted to attend the service but had been too ill. She had received medicine from a doctor that caused her to sleep during the time of the service. She reported no awareness of being out of her body. This case is well documented, and four people who knew her signed statements, as did the doctor and members of her family who were home while she was sick.[4]

Another case involved a Mr. W. P. Herbert who reported that he had once projected to the home of a friend who lived in Kenya, to a house which he had never visited. "While projected there, I could see the house and everything about it. . . . When the two little girls were observing me, their mother called and asked what they were doing. 'Looking at Nunkie,' was the reply. And they certainly were. They were looking right at me. They could not seem to understand how I got there. . . . When I later wrote to my friends, I described the house into which I had been projected and how I had seen the little girls; they wrote back that my description of the arrangements of the rooms, the windows, etc., was very accurate. They even sent me a photograph to show me the unusual window over the veranda which I described."[5]

Level 4: The most convincing evidence comes from rare cases in which the person projecting is not only seen, but accomplishes something in front of the witnesses. Sometimes an object is moved, a sleeper is awakened, a message is given, or a conversation occurs. Here is a modern case involving a twentieth-century Capuchin monk in Italy, Fr. Pio. The Roman Catholic Church has carefully researched and documented this case and is very cautious, even skeptical, in accepting such reports as valid.

General Luigi Cadorna was a commander in the Italian army in World War I. Having suffered a number of defeats, he was severely depressed and decided to kill himself and ordered the guard to let no one into his tent. While holding the pistol to his head, he saw a monk enter who looked at him for a moment and said, "Such an action is foolish"; then the monk left. The commander put down his gun and wondered who this strange monk was and how he had entered the tent. General Cadorna had never seen Padre Pio, but after the war he heard about the priest and decided to pay him a visit. When he saw the monk, he recognized him as the mysterious visitor who had prevented a suicide.[6]

A final case involved a Mrs. Riggs who reported it in a letter. "I . . . was prepared to undergo a very serious operation. I was flat on my back and could not move—could not help myself in any way. . . . One day another patient was brought in, operated upon, and placed in a ward some distance from me. . . . Her moans were pitiful and during the night I felt I wanted to go to her and say something to comfort her. *I felt myself leave my body.* I left that body in the bed and went down the ward to her side.... I told the sister about it later on, and she was very interested and said she would take me to see the other patient when I was able to go. . . .When she did so ... the woman said: 'Oh— ... I know you—you are the one who came in here to cheer me up that night after the operation when I was so ill.'... It seems so very strange. I hope my letter is of interest to you."[7]

What Can We Make of These Cases?

Level 1 cases are frequently dismissed as nothing but the effects of drugs, physical or mental illness, dreams, or hallucinations. Yet we have seen in the chapters on near-death experiences and deathbed visions that, even with these cases, there are serious problems if we try use the "nothing but" explanations. In cases of levels 2, 3, and 4, the conventional theories simply do not explain the extraordinary events that are reported. Telepathy and clairvoyance (distant seeing) are sometimes offered as explanations of this kind of event. But if it is true that the projecting person is seen in the place she or he claims to be projected, or gives accurate descriptions of places he or she has never been, or if

> How believable do you find the report by Mrs. Riggs? Why or why not? How believable do you find the church case reported by Stead? Form four groups to evaluate the four different levels of evidence. What could be a fifth level of evidence? (How could an event be even more convincing?) If anyone has shared an OBE event or report of an OBE event, under what level of evidence does it fall? What connections do you see between such experiences and life after death?

Padre Pio appears and gives a message at a place distant from his body, then mysterious events are happening indeed. In order to discount cases of this type, some may insist on fraud. Considering that there are hundreds of documented cases, fraud seems unlikely in all cases.

What If OBEs Are Dreams in Which People Become Temporarily Psychic?

There is some evidence that the simpler OBEs may be dream experiences. Dreamers and OBEers do show rapid eye movement, body paralysis, irregular pulse and blood pressure readings, and low voltage

> List every image, art work, song, movie, TV program the group can think of that suggests some out-of-body event. (Hints: angels, the song "Stairway to Heaven," the movie, *The Sixth Sense,* paintings by great religious painters, the hymn, "Nearer, My God, to Thee," stanza 5.) Let someone in the group who can draw be the scribe. With ideas from the group, let the scribe, on a chalkboard, white board, or sheet of paper, make drawings to indicate the various characteristics (above) of the OBE.

nonsynchronized EEG activity. But a striking difference between dreams and OBEs is that hundreds of people, many of whom never heard of the OBE before their experience, give reports of similar events and similar sequences of events. When there are similar patterns reported independently, it is reasonable to conclude that we are dealing with something more than coincidence.

Some common elements in OBEs are these:

1. The release of the spirit often starts at the feet, and the projected spiritual body emerges from the head. Cave paintings in France also sometimes show the spirit body as emerging from the chest or mouth.

2. The projected body is described as self-luminous and sometimes connected to the physical body by a luminous cord. (See Ecclesiastes 12:6.)

3. There is often a feeling of energy flowing in the body.

4. Sometimes there is a clicking sound or a mental blackout.

5. There are reported visions and meetings with living friends, and with dead friends, as in NDEs and DBVs.

6. Noises and vibrational sensations are reported as in the Ezekiel and Revelation passages quoted at the beginning of this chapter.

7. OBEers almost uniformly report that their consciousness is more lucid than normal consciousness and that impressions of the environment are extremely vivid.

8. OBEers almost always become convinced that there is a life after the death of the body. After all, if the spirit can leave the body before death, why not after death?

Laboratory Research on OBEs

Here we can offer only a brief summary of a very large body of research. Charles Tart reported on his work with a young woman whom he calls Miss Z. Miss Z reported having had OBEs since she was a child. Tart connected electrodes to her head to measure brain wave frequencies, and observed her for four nights in his sleep laboratory. Each night he placed a slip of paper with five digits written on it on a high shelf out of her vision, next to a clock. The electrodes on her head measured not only brainwave frequencies, but would also tell him if Miss Z tried to cheat by rising from her bed to look at the numbers. She did not attempt to cheat, but the first three nights were unproductive. On the fourth night Miss Z correctly reported the five-digit sequence (25132) on the slip of paper, and the time of her brainwave patterns marking the OBE matched the time she reported seeing on the clock while she was "out." Tart calculated that the odds of such a correct answer being given by chance are 100,000 to 1.[8] Another OBEer is reported by the American Society for Psychical Research (ASPR) as having caused lights to go on and off in the ASPR lab at the same time as he reported that he had projected to the laboratory.[9] A different subject at the ASPR correctly observed pictures through a hole in a box that were generated by a random numbers generator, so that even the experimenters did not know which pictures were being shown.[10] In at least one laboratory, animals have reacted strangely at the precise time the OBEer claimed to have been visiting the animals.[11]

> How convincing do you find these summaries of laboratory efforts to document the OBE? Do your own experiment. Let the class leader, before anyone else arrives for class, conceal a small object somewhere in the room out of sight of anyone in the group. It is best if the object relates to human love or caring and has emotional overtones, such as a piece of jewelry, a photograph, or is somehow emotionally striking. Do not use a pencil or a book or anything boring. Tell class members what area of the room the object is in, then challenge them to (out-of-body) travel there and see what the object is. Have them write down what they saw before discussing. Many groups have people who are very good at this, sometimes scoring a perfect "hit." If there are "hits" or somewhat accurate reports, discuss how we might know whether the reporter is "out-of-body," whether he or she plucked it from the leader's mind by telepathy, or it was just coincidence. How did people feel during the experiment?

What Conclusions Fit With Biblical Reports, Case Studies, and Laboratory Findings?

The central question seems to be whether a "spirit" or a "something" actually leaves the physical body. We know that some drugs, especially ketamine, will trigger OBEs. We can reasonably suspect that some OBE reports are drug-induced or are elaborations of dream experiences. Yet the evidence from Scripture, from case studies of NDEs, DBVs and OBEs, from cross-cultural observations and laboratory studies seems to suggest that OBEs may be the result of other factors. Scripture and research both suggest that in some instances something like a spirit or spiritual body actually leaves the physical body at death and sometimes before death. This fits well with Paul's view, outlined in the introduction of this book, that there is a physical body and there is a spiritual body. Here we begin to see more clearly the convergence of the biblical view and the modern research discoveries. This is one place where science and Scripture support one another, in powerful ways.

Many New Testament passages indicate that Jesus and the early church believed that a spiritual body goes out of the physical body. These ideas are not simply "thought patterns of biblical times" but are related to human experiences in all places and in all times in history. Here are just a few examples:

What do you think are the attitudes of people in our rather materialistic culture toward experiences such as the OBE? What is the difference between "a thought pattern of biblical times" and a belief based on actual experience? How might this research on OBEs provide support for spiritual conversations with people you know? What, if any, effect have you noticed in your own spiritual life as a result of this study on life after death? What new dimensions, if any, do you think the OBE and the research on it can add to your faith?

"We shall not all sleep." (1 Corinthians 15:51, RSV)

"Today you will be with me in Paradise." (Luke 23:43)

"Do not fear those who kill the body but cannot kill the soul." (Matthew 10:28, RSV)

"This night your soul is required of you." (Luke 12:20, RSV)

"The Lord has risen indeed, and has appeared to Simon!" (Luke 24:34, RSV)

How Are OBEs to Be "Used"?

This OBE shows the great affection of a husband for his wife, who had fainted in the bathtub. She was floating face down. The husband was in another room reading, and she reportedly left her body and tapped him on the shoulder. He was apparently not consciously aware of her presence, but felt compelled to go into the bathroom. Seeing his wife in the water, he pulled her out and gave her artificial respiration. When she recovered, the wife reported that she was watching him during the entire process.[12] This report, like most of the other examples given in this chapter, shows the OBE occurring in the context of spiritual experience or in caring human or animal interactions. The OBE is something to be deeply respected and is worthy of thoughtful exploration. It is regarded by some as a spiritual gift. Again, OBEers almost always become convinced of life after the death of the body, so the experience is very powerful and has the capacity to bring permanent spiritual and life changes for those who receive it.

Closing
   Give thanks for the OBE as yet another strand of evidence that supports a view of life that includes spirit. Give thanks for further evidence that challenges a materialistic view of life and that offers a way beyond the moral uncertainty that often accompanies such a view.

Notes

1. From *Beyond the Body,* by Susan Blackmore (Chicago: Academy Chicago Publishers, 1982); pages 85–87.
2. From *You Cannot Die,* by Ian Currie (Toronto: Somerville House, 1998); pages 115–21.
3. From *The Astral Journey,* by Herbert Greenhouse (New York: Doubleday and Company, 1975); page 42.
4. From *The Astral Journey;* page 85.
5. From *You Cannot Die;* page 119.
6. From *The Astral Journey;* page 82.
7. From *You Cannot Die;* page 121.
8. From *Body Mind Spirit,* edited by Charles T. Tart (Hampton Roads Publishing Co., 1997); pages 178–79.

9. From *The Astral Journey;* pages 281–82.
10. From *The Astral Journey;* pages 289–90.
11. From *The Astral Journey;* page 297–98.
12. From *The Astral Journey;* page 119.

For More Information
Internet Key Words—Type the following words and phrases into an Internet search program for additional information.

Christian Out-of-Body Experience
Parapsychology and Personal Survival After Death
Out-of-Body Experience Research Foundation

CHAPTER 4
APPARITIONS

"That very day two of them were going to a village named Emmaus, about seven miles from Jerusalem, and talking with each other about all these things that had happened. While they were talking and discussing together, Jesus himself drew near and went with them. But their eyes were kept from recognizing him. . . . So they drew near to the village to which they were going. He appeared to be going further, but they constrained him, saying, 'Stay with us, for it is toward evening and the day is far spent.' So he went in to stay with them. When he was at table with them, he took the bread and blessed, and broke it, and gave it to them. And their eyes were opened and they recognized him; and he vanished out of their sight."

—Luke 24:13-16, 28-31, RSV

Modern Apparitions Research

The study of apparitions is central in our exploration of life after death. Highly trained scientific people have been studying apparitions for many decades. Yet, the existence of this material is one of the best kept secrets in our materialistic society. Most people will be surprised to learn that

> **Focus:** This chapter explores modern reports of apparitions and invites learners to compare and contrast such reports to biblical accounts of the post-Resurrection appearances of Jesus and the promise of our own resurrection.

modern research goes very far beyond the "ghost stories" that have entertained all of us. Since few people know about apparitions research, we begin with some definitions.

> **Gathering**
> Greet one another. Tell about a story, a TV show, a movie, or an experience of seeing an apparition. What feelings or thoughts do you have about apparitions? Think about ways they do or do not relate to your understanding of life after death. Pray for God's guidance as you explore reports of apparitions.

1. *An Apparition Experience* "... is awareness of the presence of a personal being whose physical body is not in the area of the experiencer, provided the experiencer is sane and in a normal waking state of consciousness.... Apparitions are experienced as part of the immediate real world and cannot be readily created, altered or terminated at will, except by physical actions such as closing the eyes, running away, or hiding under bedcovers."[1]

2. *A Veridical Apparition* gives information, previously unknown to the observer, that can subsequently be verified. This kind of event cannot be repeated at will but is extremely convincing to persons witnessing it and of great interest to researchers.

3. *An Anecdotal Report* is a report that cannot be repeated or verified. There are thousands of such reports. They occur in different periods of history, different cultures, and to adherents of different religions.

Some Statistics

In 1987, Andrew Greeley conducted a poll for the National Opinion Research Center. In the poll he found that "42% of American adults believe they have been in contact with someone who has died. And 67% of all widows believe they have had a similar experience."[2] These encounters may involve one or several of the senses: feeling, seeing, hearing, smelling, being touched by, and talking to the presence. Other polls in the U.S. and England yield similar statistics. Frederick Myers found that when two or more people are present, two-thirds of the time two or more people will experience the apparition.[3] Ian Stevenson found that 52 percent of reported apparitional events followed a violent or sudden death.[4]

Different Kinds of Apparitions

1. *Crisis apparitions* are the most common form of veridical apparitions and are so striking that they are almost never forgotten. There are thousands of such cases. A Mrs. Paquet woke up feeling strangely depressed and prepared for herself a cup of tea. "I turned around [and saw] my brother Edmund [standing] only a few feet away ... with his back toward m ... [he] was in the act of falling forward—away from me— seemingly impelled by two loops ... of rope drawing against his legs. [In] a moment, [he disappeared] over a low railing or bulwark ... I dropped

the tea, clasped my hands to my face, and exclaimed, 'My God! Ed is drowned!' "[5] As it turned out, Mrs. Paquet's brother had died, six hours earlier on a ship, in the way she had seen in the apparitional event.

2. *Collectively perceived apparitions* happen when two or more people see a similar figure in the same place, at the same time. Most of the post-Resurrection appearances were of this type. A young English couple were settling into bed for the evening. Suddenly the young woman saw, standing at the foot of the bed, a man dressed as a naval officer. She was astonished because she knew that the doors were locked, and nothing had alerted them that someone would be entering the house. She reported that she was too astonished to be afraid, and, touching her husband's shoulder, asked, "Willie, who is this?" The husband turned, was astonished, and asked, "What on earth are you doing here, sir?" The figure replied, "Willie! Willie!" and slowly moved toward the wall. The room became dark, according to the wife, like a room when someone passes in front of a lamp, then the figure disappeared into the wall. The husband, very agitated, searched the house, then came back, shaken, to the bedroom. "Do you know what we have seen?... It was my father!" The father had been dead fourteen years.[6]

3. *Apparitions of the dead* are events that occur more than twelve hours after the death.

This important case was investigated by the American Society for Psychical Research and widely reported in the research on apparitions. An elderly man named Chaffin had been dead for about four years. One of his sons had dreams on a number of occasions in which his father appeared at his bedside. On the last occasion, the apparition appeared wearing Mr. Chaffin's old black overcoat and informed his son that in the pocket of his old overcoat was a (previously unknown) second will. The son found the will, and it was admitted to probate in 1928 in Davie County, North Carolina.[7]

> What are your own thoughts about these modern apparition reports? Which are more believable, or less believable? How might you respond if you had an apparitional experience? Write a short poem or paragraph about how your life would be different if you experienced an apparition. Write words that fit a familiar tune to express your beliefs about life after death.

"A personal example of an apparition of the dead happened in my family, following the death of my eighteen-year-old son, Mark." One of

Mark's siblings reported a dream at the breakfast table: "I dreamed Mark and I were eating peanut butter sandwiches in the kitchen. I asked him, 'How did you get out of your body?' He said, 'When I got to the yellow doors, there were two of me and I took a new body.' " We knew that the body had been picked up by the mortician after the accident in a town 200 miles away, but we had not gone there; rather, we had the body brought to our hometown by the local mortician. Having read some of the near-death reports about a separation of body and spirit, I wrote the mortician and asked if he had any yellow doors. He wrote back and sent photographs. The van that picked up the body was shown with its back doors open—they were bright yellow.

4. *Haunting apparitions* are the stuff of ghost stories and everyone has heard such tales. There are many such reports that have been carefully investigated by the American and British Societies for Psychical Research and other responsible scientific groups. Media presentations do not reflect the prudence and caution with which some research is done. As with the other types of apparitions, it is far wiser to study the reports carefully rather than to dismiss them out of hand.

Characteristics of Apparitions

Apparitions have both "physical" features and "nonphysical" features, sometimes occurring in the same event. These observations are based on reviewing thousands of apparitional reports. Physical features: In modern reports there is often an opaqueness that is reflected in mirrors. Apparitions adapt to situations by approaching or withdrawing from people present, walking around physical objects, and sometimes being walked around. They are seen from different perspectives by different people. On rare occasions they move objects, and electric gadgets are sometimes switched on or off.

> What thoughts or feelings do you have about the characteristics of apparitions as described in the various reports?

Sometimes animals react to apparitions. And apparitions wear clothes!

Nonphysical features: Apparitions at times glide rather than walk, and sometimes go through walls or doors. They sometimes just appear, rather than making a normal approach. They are seen by some people and not by others and are not always recognized; or, as in the story about the appearance of Jesus on the road to Emmaus, only recognized later. Then, he "vanished" (Luke 24:31). Modern apparitions also vanish.

Several Theories About Apparitions

The *"hallucination"* theory does not suggest mental illness. Many researchers believe that the deceased person somehow triggers a "hallucination" or vision in a normal person or group. This requires that observers receive telepathic messages from the deceased. This theory works for some types of events, such as that in which the apparition is wearing clothes. According to this theory the percipient receives the message from the deceased, then "rounds out" the experience by mentally creating clothes for the apparition to wear! With veridical apparitions, this theory assumes that the deceased can give through telepathy a verifiable message, such as the message about the will in the Chaffin case and the message about the yellow doors in the Mark Hover case.

> **Create a Skit**
>
> You are deceased and are together with a group of deceased people. You all want to reassure your loved ones that you are all right. Think of ways you could try to communicate; then put your ideas into the form of a skit.

A serious problem with this theory is that very few people display any great telepathic ability, and such events seem to require a talent that can only be considered as Super ESP.

The *"spirit"* theory was developed because the "hallucination" theory does not explain all apparitional events. For example, some apparitions show a sense of purpose. Are we to think that apparitions convey a sense of purpose by telepathy? Also, collective apparitions are not easily explained by the "hallucination" theory. Are we to think that people receive a message by telepathy as to which side of the apparition they are to stand or the different perspectives from which they see the apparition? The "hallucination" theory also does not work well with "haunting" cases. There are well-documented cases in which the same apparition seems to afflict several different owners of the house, at different times. Are we to think that all of this information is transmitted to generations of residents by ESP?

The "spirit" theory seems better to many researchers. These researchers believe that "something" actually leaves the body of the deceased and that it has a physical or semi-physical quality. With purposeful apparitions, it seems more reasonable to think that "something" is acting with a purpose. With collective apparitions, it seems simpler to think that "something" is actually present in the group, whose members see it from different perspectives, or sometimes not at all.

This "something" has been called soul or spirit in many different religions and cultures. Paul called it a "spiritual body" in 1 Corinthians 15. He distinguished it from a physical body. Other passages, especially in the Gospel of John, give an impression of a physical presence of the risen Lord. Hence, we have at least two strands of thinking in the New Testament and some controversy among Christian believers.

Resurrection in Christian Faith

Resurrection is the heart of Christian faith. For the scientific mind, the Resurrection seems to be such an astonishing and unbelievable event that it seems not a great deal more than this can be said about it except that the early Christians were convinced that Jesus rose from the dead. This popular view does not go nearly far enough, and the whole issue has been most difficult for modern theologians as well as for pastors and laypersons.

Modern apparition research may expand and energize our view of Jesus' resurrection and thoughts about our own resurrection. The New Testament reports that Jesus rose from the dead and appeared to many. The post-Resurrection appearances of Jesus also happened to people who were emotionally close to him. They involved people feeling a presence, seeing a presence, hearing a presence, talking to the presence, and touching the presence. Most appearances happened in groups, and they occurred after Jesus had suffered a violent death. There are other similarities as well, but it seems clear that a careful study of apparition research offers ways of thinking that can help us understand these strange New Testament reports.

The Post-Resurrection Appearances

In 1 Corinthians 15, Paul reports that Jesus was seen by Peter, then by the Twelve, then by 500 at once, by James, then by all the apostles, finally by Paul himself. According to Luke, chapter 24, the women who had accompanied Jesus to the tomb were the first to see him on Easter; then two of the disciples saw Jesus on the road to Emmaus; then he was seen by all the disciples. Matthew 28 reports that Jesus was seen by Mary Magdalene and the other Mary, then in Galilee by the eleven disciples. John 20 and 21 reports that he appeared to Mary Magdalene, to the disciples, again to the disciples, then to the disciples at the Sea of Tiberias.

Thoughtful people will recognize that there are not many options in interpreting these reports. One is that Jesus' body was stolen and disposed of, the disciples and Mary were hallucinating or deceitful, and the Resurrection faith is based on an illusion. This would suggest too that the post-Resurrection reports are literary fabrications. Another is that the appearances were so intensely real that they caused the disciples and early Christians to exert enormous effort to spread the report of resurrection and to be willing to die in claiming it to be true. In our time, it is probably impossible to understand the risks involved for early Christians in confessing faith in the risen Christ.

> **Bible Study**
> Form four groups. One group will read and discuss Paul's report in 1 Corinthians 15, the second group will read Luke 24, a third Matthew 28, and the last group will read John 20 and 21.
> Return to the whole group, and report about the Resurrection from each Scripture. What are the differences in the reports? Which of the appearances sound more "physical"? more "spiritual"? Where did they occur? What was the reported impact on those who saw Jesus? What feelings do you have as you read through these passages? What thoughts?

Several Different Views of Resurrection

One outlook influenced a number of important theologians in the more liberal churches in the nineteenth and twentieth centuries. Rising from the work of Feuerbach and Freud and later psychoanalysts, this view is that religion is largely a product of anxiety or wishful thinking. The disciples were simply reporting subjective visions or hallucinations if they were not lying. In this view, faith comes from our

> Which of these views fits best with your own beliefs? Which matches your temperament best? Which views are represented, do you think, by members of your congregation? by your friends?

admiration and emulation of Jesus, but not from the presence of the risen Lord, except in our minds.

> As a group, make a list or collection of images or symbols that suggest resurrection, eternal life, or immortality. For example, the cross, the fish, the bird, the butterfly.

A more conservative approach is linked to the Hebrew idea of a resurrection of the body in the last days. There is a physical quality in Old Testament ideas of resurrection. This is reflected in John's account of Jesus showing the disciples his hands and his side and inviting them to eat fish. This has been called an "objective" view of the post-Resurrection appearances.

Another view has been labeled the "visionary" view of the post-Resurrection appearances. Paul's and Matthew's reports reflect an episode quite different from a physical-like presence. The writers use words like "They saw him," "He came to them," "He appeared." This account is more acceptable for some modern Christians—that a seeing, or a vision, or an appearance can be triggered by the real presence of the risen Lord. This notion also seems to fit with Paul's distinction between an earthly body and a spiritual body (1 Corinthians 15:35-44). Presumably, from this point of view, when Jesus "appeared" it was in his spiritual body.

Difficulties

Whatever idea we hold presents difficulties. If the Resurrection was physical, then what about the passages from Paul and Matthew? If it was spiritual, how do we interpret the passages in John's Gospel? The answer may be that there were different kinds of events, some more "physical" and some more "spiritual." It is worth noting that the biblical record of both the physical and the spiritual aspects of the post-Resurrection appearances and of the

> What is your judgment about taking the Resurrection on "faith" versus doing research on apparitions to see if the post-Resurrection reports and modern apparitional reports have any connections?

expectations regarding our own resurrections correlates with modern research on apparitions. This opens new horizons for agreement among conservative and liberal Christians and among those who wish to think in more scientific, even psychological and parapsychological terms.

A Powerful Argument

Experience is a powerful and convincing source for knowledge. But when experience, science, reason, and authority point in the same direction, we have a powerful argument indeed.

Some people are willing to discount all of the research results as wishful thinking, illusions, or lies, and in the same way to discount the reports of Jesus' post-Resurrection appearances. However, this requires a great deal of discounting! Others will conclude that

> **Organize a Debate**
> *Side 1:* There is no reason to expect a life after death. When you're dead, you're dead.
> *Side 2:* There are defensible reasons to believe that Jesus rose from the dead and that we also will rise.

there is substantial evidence that Jesus did indeed rise from the dead and that he continues to be present with us in exactly the ways that the church has always insisted. The theology of the Resurrection grew, not from the cleverness and imaginations of theologians, but from actual encounters of people with the risen Christ. Modern people also encounter the deceased; otherwise veridical and collective apparitional events simply would not happen. We believe there is a solid basis for a confidence in life after death and that, like the figures in apparitional experiences and like Jesus, we will also be raised to Life.

> **Closing**
> Close with a prayer for understanding and guidance, and for clear thinking to sort out the difficult issues about apparitions, the post-Resurrection appearances of Jesus, and the promises of our own resurrection. Give thanks for the promise of eternal life.

Notes

1. From "Life After Death?" by Karlis Osis in *Newsletter of the American Society for Psychical Research,* Summer, 1990, Vol. XVI, No. 3; page 2.

2. From *Hello From Heaven!* by Bill and Judy Guggenheim (Bantam Books, New York, 1997); page 12.

3. From "The Contribution of Apparitions to the Evidence for Survival,"

by Ian Stevenson in *Journal of the American Society for Psychical Research* (New York, October 1982, Volume 76, Number 4); page 349.

4. From "The Contribution of Apparitions to the Evidence for Survival"; page 347.

5. From *You Cannot Die,* by Ian Currie (Somerville House, Toronto, 1998); page 21.

6 From *You Cannot Die;* pages 35, 36.

7. From *Aristocracy of the Dead,* by Arthur S. Berger (McFarland & Company, Inc., Jefferson, North Carolina, 1987); page 165.

For More Information
Internet Key Words—Type the following words and phrases into an Internet search program for additional information:

Parapsychology and Survival After Death
Apparitions and Survival of Death
The Problem of Survival
Jesus' Post-Resurrection Appearances

Internet Links—Use the following Internet addresses for additional information:

http://survivalafterdeath.org/experiments/other/apparitions.htm
http://survivalafterdeath.org/articles.htm
the-atlantic-paranormal-society.com/ [choose "investigators"]
victorzammit.com

CHAPTER 5
REINCARNATION

"Now when Jesus came into the district of Caesarea Philippi, he asked his disciples, 'Who do people say that the Son of man is?' And they said, 'Some say John the Baptist, but others Elijah, and still others Jeremiah or one of the prophets.'"

—Matthew 16:13-14

A Definition

In this chapter, we define *reincarnation* as a belief that life does not end at death but is transformed into other forms. Other words used to express somewhat different versions of this idea are *transmigration* and *metempsychosis*. All three words express the concept that after death, the essential living principle of an entity is reborn in a new body. In the common understanding of reincarnation, a soul enters a body, sometimes has memories of previous lives, may have birthmarks from earlier bodies, and has to deal with old problems carried over from other lives. In Hinduism and Buddhism, as well as the various Islamic and tribal ideas of reincarnation, there are many variations on this theme. Eastern ideas

Focus: This chapter will focus on the history of reincarnation thinking, the modern research on reincarnation, and how reincarnation ideas do or do not fit with Christian beliefs.

What is your understanding of reincarnation? How many of your friends, family, or acquaintances have expressed interest or belief in some form of reincarnation?

Gathering
Think about the various topics we have studied so far and your feelings about what you have learned. Pray for God's guidance as you open your mind and spirit to explore reincarnation.

generally highlight the need to live an ethical life in order to get off the endless cycle of rebirths. Western ideas are more optimistic, considering repeated lives as opportunities to learn and grow, with the hope of eventual salvation.

A Not-so-Foreign Idea

The encounter between Christian and reincarnation thinking gives us a good opportunity to understand both in a deeper and more personal way. Many people sense this and are eager to learn and talk about the subject.

> Tell about your first impression of the meaning of Matthew 16:13-14. What connections, if any, do you make between this Scripture and reincarnation? What surprises, if any, have you encountered in the reading of this chapter so far? What is your first thought about whether reincarnation and Christian faith are compatible?

The New Testament neither confirms nor denies reincarnation, and reincarnation has never been a formal part of Christian doctrine. Surprisingly, most major polls, including several Gallup Polls, show that at least 25 percent of Americans believe in reincarnation.[1] The belief certainly is linked to the issue of what happens after we die and is one way in which hundreds of millions of people conceive of life after death. Reincarnation also

> Find a partner. Talk about a life event that caused you to wonder about reincarnation.

offers a reply to the problem of evil by teaching that suffering comes from human failures and not from acts of reprisal by God. Moreover, it is not exact to say that reincarnation is an idea that is foreign to the church. Grim battles were fought about it in the early and later centuries of Christian history, with some important early theologians teaching reincarnation of a

> Collect from the Internet or from a library examples of Christian, Hindu, or Buddhist poetry, art, or music that suggest each religion's views of life after death. How are the views different? the same?

Christian sort. Whether we discover that reincarnation beliefs can or cannot fit into a Christian view, Christians do well to become familiar with the issues if we wish to take part in modern discussions on spirituality. We will examine three areas as an introduction to this topic: past life regression in psychotherapy, investigations of children's memories of past lives, and Christian faith and reincarnation beliefs.

Past Life Regression in Psychotherapy

The recent swell of interest in past life regression in the U.S. was spurred by Morey Bernstein's experiments, written up in 1956 as the famous Bridey Murphy case. Psychiatrists and psychologists have for some time been using hypnotic past life regression as a way to detect and unravel problems brought to them by patients.

On the whole, therapists are much less concerned with reincarnation than with using past life regressions to help patients. Some therapists even tell their patients that a belief in reincarnation is not necessary for past life therapy to be effective. The field has grown and there are now professional journals for past life therapists, training programs, and an Association for Past Life Research and Therapy.

Roger J. Woolger, Ph.D., one of the more persuasive of the past life therapists, gave this account: A professional woman in her forties was having considerable anxiety about leaving her cats alone in her city apartment. The worry was so great that she had not been able to take vacations, and her fretfulness seemed far out of proportion to any actual happenings related to her pets. In hypnosis, she reported a tragic story. She was living in a bleak stone house, and there was a storm outside. She had been fighting with her husband, who had said that she did not care about the children. The husband was screaming outside, had the children there, and she would not let them in. After all became quiet, she heard a knocking and believed that her husband had sent the little boy to plead with his mother, but she did not relent. In the morning, when the storm was over and they did not come back, she assumed that the husband had taken them to an inn. Opening the door, she discovered her daughter dead and her son unconscious. She learned that the husband had struggled to take the children to an inn, but had died of a heart attack. The children had come back to the house, but she had not let them in, and eventually the little boy also died. She had never told her neighbors and had lived with the guilt for the rest of her life, never trusting herself to take care of anyone again.[2] Woolger reports that at the end of the session the woman was greatly relieved and shortly afterward was able to take a two-week vacation, had a wonderful time, and never thought about her cats. If true, this is an astonishing case, but no more so than the hundreds of other cases that could be reported.

Carol Bowman, another therapist, tells of a therapy case involving a three-year-old boy named Blake. One morning Blake was standing near the door watching his older brother as he waited outside for the school bus. Suddenly Blake shouted, "Get out of the street, the bus is coming!" Colleen, Blake's mother, checked to see that Trevor was all right, and Blake said, with his hand to his head, "My ear hurts." Colleen asked why his ear hurt, and Blake said, "A truck hit me." He insisted that it was not a toy truck but "a big truck," then told her that he had been hurt in the street, gone under the wheels of a big truck, and had been taken to a "school." Asked where his parents were when this happened, he said, "Gone bye-bye at the store." Then Colleen asked if he had died, and he simply answered, "Yes." Later that week, he spontaneously told his mother that he had been hit by a garbage truck. His personality seemed gradually to change and he became depressed, angry with his parents, and complained of physical symptoms: a sore arm, a sore leg, always on the left side of his body, and indicated he wanted to be run over by a truck. Colleen consulted a therapist and asked how best to respond to the story Blake was telling and that seemed so genuine to him. One evening she asked again if he had been hit by a truck. When he said yes, she explained to him that he had been hit by a truck in a different life than this and that he had a different mommy and daddy and a different body. She told him that everyone in his family loved and cared for him very much. Colleen reported that his face lit up, the depression and physical symptoms disappeared almost immediately, and Blake again became his happy little-boy self. Bowman believes that Blake was confusing his past-life parents with his present-life parents, hence the love and hate, and the depression and confusion.[3]

> How believable do you find these reports to be? What do you find believable or doubtful about them? Which, if any, of the comments made by skeptics seem any more reasonable than a belief in reincarnation?

Are These Cases "Real"?

There are hundreds, even thousands, of similar cases; and it is not reasonable to dismiss all of them. However, critics may wonder whether there are explanations other than past life that would clarify the events.

Some prefer to think that people are extremely creative and may, with help, fashion scenarios to heal themselves more effectively than happens in ordinary therapy or ordinary life. Others believe that there is a kind of "universal consciousness" in which all things are recorded and that patients and others somehow attune to that consciousness.

Investigations of Children's Memories of Past Lives

Ian Stevenson, a recently retired psychiatrist, spent much of his life teaching at the University of Virginia Medical School and doing scientific research on reincarnation. His work is detailed, voluminous, and difficult to follow. Tom Schroder and Carol Bowman have made his work more easily accessible to the wider public. Stevenson is highly respected even by those who do not agree with his belief that reincarnation is the best explanation for the many strange cases he has studied. Through the years he has collected and investigated several hundred cases of children who claim to remember past lives. In each case, he has checked their reports to see if they reflect actual events about which the children could have no normal knowledge. Recently, Stevenson has published *Where Reincarnation and Biology Intersect*, a study of birth marks in children who claim past life memories. Most of his cases are from cultures where there is a belief in reincarnation, but there are also a number of American cases in families where reincarnation was probably never discussed.

Victor Vincent was a full blooded Tlingit (Eskimo) who lived in Alaska and died in 1946. Tlingits believe in reincarnation and that if a woman has a dream of a deceased relative that relative will reincarnate in her child. If there are birthmarks on the child that reflect injuries to the previous person, the matter is settled. One day, on a visit to his niece, Mrs. Corliss Chotkin, Victor announced that he was coming back as her next son. He hoped that he would not stutter and said that he would have birthmarks to match two scars he had from earlier operations. Eighteen months later, Mrs. Chotkin gave birth to a boy who had birthmarks of the same shape in the same places on his body as those of Victor Vincent. The child spontaneously said, "I'm Kahkody," which was the tribal name Victor Vincent had used. At age two, the boy recognized a stepdaughter of Victor Vincent and called her by her correct name. At age two, he saw a son of Victor Vincent's and said, "There is William, my son." On another occasion he picked Victor Vincent's widow out of a crowd and said, "That's the old lady" and "That's

Have two people volunteer to roleplay. One person is a small child reporting presumed memories of a past life. The other person is a grandmother or grandfather to whom the child is speaking. The grandparent may ask questions. What are your initial thoughts after reading the summaries of the cases above? How possible is it to rule out fraud in cases like Victor Vincent's? In general, how likely are you to accept new ideas from people whom you don't know?

Rose." Stevenson reports that her name was Rose and that he was told that Victor indeed referred to her as "the old lady." He narrated several events in Victor Vincent's life, which his mother believed he had never heard. One had to do with Victor's having put on a Salvation Army uniform to attract attention from a passing ship when his boat engine was broken down. In another, the boy recognized a house Victor had visited and noted in which room he and Rose had stayed, even though the house had undergone extensive remodeling.[4]

We have here summarized in one paragraph over ten pages of Stevenson's report. This is one of several hundreds of cases he has investigated, many written in far more detail than this one. Stevenson's central interest is to rule out the possibility of the children receiving knowledge through normal channels of information. He believes that in a handful of his cases, including this one, reincarnation is the simplest and most reasonable explanation. It is not reasonable to dismiss all of his cases. His work is detailed and difficult; but for many of those who read it, it is very persuasive. On the other hand, a person might ask several questions. How can we rule out fraud? How can we rule out the child's receiving information by telepathy from the deceased, or even from the living who remember the life of the deceased? If the child has information regarding the life of a deceased person, why would we conclude that therefore she is that person? These are important questions.

Organize a panel discussion. Four people read and form a panel for the next group meeting. Two of the people will read what they can find of Bowman and Stevenson's material and argue in favor of a reincarnationist view. The other two people read the same kind of material and argue against a reincarnationist view.

Christian Faith and Reincarnation

Most theologians and biblical scholars argue against trying to fit reincarnation ideas into Christian belief, but some argue for it. Several respected theologians have struggled to offer balanced comments on these concerns, including Geddes MacGregor and John Hick. We will look at both sides of the argument.

Perhaps the best known Protestant leader who argued that reincarnation thinking is helpful to Christians was Leslie Weatherhead, a well-known Methodist minister and author in London in the mid-twentieth century. Weatherhead wrote, "The intelligent Christian asks not only that life should be just, but that it shall make sense. Does the idea of reincarnation help here? I think it does.... How can a world progress in inner things—which are the most important—if the birth of every new generation fills the world with unregenerate souls full of original sin? There can never be a perfect world unless gradually those born into it can take advantage of the lessons learned in earlier lives instead of starting at scratch."[5] The argument is not this simple, so we will look at a wider range of questions.

Does the New Testament Support Reincarnation?

Protestant theologian John Hick outlines several of the concerns Christian people have about reincarnation and tries to address them in a balanced manner.[6]

Some Christians believe that the passage quoted from Matthew at the beginning of this chapter is only one of many that support a belief in reincarnation—that since Jesus did not argue with the disciples' comments that people thought he was John the Baptist, Elijah, or Jeremiah, he must have agreed with those comments. But careful study of the New Testament in its Jewish context shows that many believed that Elijah had not died but was taken into heaven in a whirlwind (2 Kings 2:11) and would return one day to prepare the way for the messiah. So this passage probably does not reflect reincarnation thinking. Other passages that have been used to support reincarnation are Matthew 17:9-13; Matthew 11:7-15; John 6:62; John 8:56-59; John 1:14-15; and Ephesians 1:4.

Challenging the Whole Pattern of Salvation?

Some Christians believe reincarnation defies the whole pattern of salvation. Christian faith places great importance on the present life and the time frame of the present life in which salvation or punishment are to occur. Others believe that the focus of salvation is on growth and eternal life, not on where (or when) they occur. Salvation may occur, as some believe, in this world (reincarnation) or as some Christians believe, in another world (heaven or hell).

Reincarnation and Resurrection?

Also, reincarnation may not fit with a theology of the Resurrection, particularly a resurrection of a body, physical or spiritual. What need would there be for any kind of body if the soul is many times reincarnated? A middle ground could be that in both Christian doctrine and in reincarnation, people are given a body appropriate for life after death. This would mean that reincarnation involves resurrection of a particular kind, and Christian faith involves resurrection of another kind.

One Life, One Salvation?

Some also say that a belief in reincarnation would compromise the one-time historical event of Jesus Christ's life and death. Others say that there is no connection between the idea that Jesus Christ died one time only for the sins of the world and the idea that we have only one life in which to accept the benefit of that atonement. In this view, in responding to God's love made flesh in Jesus Christ, people could go on being reborn until they grow and learn and reach the maturity of fully accepting the benefit of that atonement.

Faith or Works?

Some Christians emphasize that God is a God of infinite mercy who chooses to offer salvation only through Jesus, as Luke wrote in Acts: "There is salvation in no one else" (4:12). Reincarnation suggests that there are many opportunities to "get it right" and that salvation may be more linked to human effort than to God's free gift in Christ.

An Active or a Passive God?

Finally, some feel that a difference between Christian and reincarnation thinking is this: God as described in Judaism and Christianity is active and involved in the world, which he created and called good. They believe that in reincarnation thinking, at least of the more philosophical Hindu type, that God's involvement seems more passive, less personal, and perhaps more distant. In terms of ethics, some think reincarnation suggests a more mystical individual and spiritual journey, where kindness to others brings one closer to God and away from the "unreal" material world. A Judeo-Christian view gives emphasis to a need for active involvement in the world and a faith that God is actively with us in a partnership for the fulfillment of God's plan. Some Christians and some Hindus would not agree that this distinction is accurate.

> Which of the issues above resonate most with your faith? least? Explain. Are the differences between Christian faith and reincarnation thinking irreconcilable, or do they seem more to be matters of emphasis? Explain your view.

To Summarize

Reincarnation is not proven and seems foreign to Christian Scripture. If research eventually verifies it as factual, then there will continue to be gradual changes in Christian beliefs to reflect the new findings. This would not be the first time church teachings have been changed to fit with new knowledge. For example, almost no one believes that the earth is the center of the universe, yet church authorities in the seventeenth century were most unhappy about Galileo's teaching that it was not. There are other examples of how Christian teaching has incorporated scientific findings. We should keep a faithful openness to new understandings from direct experience, from scriptural study, from theology, and from the sciences, including reincarnation research.

> In addition to the church's initial reaction to Galileo's teaching, what other things has the church changed its mind about on the basis of new discoveries through the centuries?

Closing
Offer a prayer of gratitude for the wisdom of the various religious traditions and of the many different personal experiences given to adherents of the faiths. Pray for gradual development of common understandings as God reveals truth to all people.

Notes

1. From "Americans' Belief in Psychic and Paranormal Phenomena Is up Over Last Decade," Gallup News Service, *http://home.sandiego.edu/~baber/logic/gallup.html.*

2. From *Other Lives, Other Selves,* by Roger J. Woolger (Bantam Books, 1987); page 96.

3. From *Children's Past Lives,* by Carol Bowman (Bantam Books, 1997); pages 167–71.

4. From *Twenty Cases Suggestive of Reincarnation,* by Ian Stevenson (University Press of Virginia, 1974); pages 259–69.

5. From *Reincarnation: The Phoenix Fire Mystery,* compiled and edited by Joseph Head and Sylvia Cranston (Theosophical University Press, 1994); pages 184–85.

6. From *Death and Eternal Life,* by John Hick (Harper and Row, 1976); pages 366–73.

For More Information
Internet Key Words—Type the following words and phrases into an Internet search program for additional information:

Reincarnation Research
Reincarnation and Christian Faith
Ian Stevenson
Christianity Reincarnation

CHAPTER 6
AFTER-DEATH COMMUNICATION

"I am not going to leave you alone in the world—I am coming to you. In a very little while, the world will see me no more but you will see me, because I am really alive and you will be alive too."

—John 14:18-19, JBP

Are Encounters With the Risen Lord Similar to Encounters With Deceased Loved Ones?

Focus: In this chapter we will examine reports of personal encounters with those who have predeceased us and who are with the risen Christ.

The Gospel writers report that Jesus continued to communicate with his people after the death of his physical body. The passage above from the Gospel of John anticipates the post-Resurrection messages of Jesus, is consistent with them, and contains a promise that Jesus will communicate with those he loves. We believe this opens the door to an investigation not only of modern direct encounters with the risen Christ but also of modern encounters with loved ones who have passed on.

After-death-communications (ADCs) is an area where there has been

---

Gathering

In a period of quietness, be open to the presence of the risen Christ in this group and of those faithful who have predeceased us. Consider ways that such encounters can support faith in life after death. Read John 14:18-21. What hope does the Scripture offer to you? What connections do you see between the Scripture and after-death communication? Give thanks that we are not alone, even when we think that we are.

great bewilderment for at least two reasons. In the last several hundred years, people in Western culture have become more materialistic, and fewer people expect a direct encounter with the risen Christ or with deceased loved ones. Some believe the Old Testament passages about communicating with the deceased forbid any attempt to communicate with loved ones who have died. Others, such as the Spiritualists, have made communication with the deceased an important part of their faith.

This chapter will review the Old Testament prohibitions, modern research on psychics (*psychic* is a modern word for *medium*), the escalating interest in ADCs, Christian ideas about the communion of saints, and some present-day reports of encounters with the risen Christ. This study can, like studies of NDEs, DBVs, OBEs, Apparitions, and the research on reincarnation, lead to a building up of faith and to a trust in life after death.

Biblical Warnings Versus Biblical Respect
for Real Psychic Experiences

Leviticus 19:31 says that we should not consult wizards or mediums. According to *The Interpreter's Dictionary of the Bible,* wizards and mediums were those who practice divination. Divination generally meant foretelling future events by gazing at objects, such as the stars, the liver of an animal, the appearances and disappearances of snakes, the howling or behaviors of dogs. Information based on these methods was labeled false prophecy, in contrast to the inspired prophecy of the Old Testament prophets. In Deuteronomy 18:10-12, the concern is the same, and a brief history is helpful. In local shrines outside the Temple, for centuries there had been practices of fertility religions. Sometimes priests and priestesses attempted to consult the dead in order to predict the future. The dead were not thought to be concerned with morality, so anything they might communicate would not be expected to be consistent with the ethical code of the Old Testament Prophets and the Ten Commandments. These concerns are perhaps like modern distrust of Juju, Voodoo, and Black Magic.

In contrast, the aim of authentic, modern psychic work is to support, not undermine, the authority and ethical teachings of God. The encounter of Saul with the witch of Endor is not so different from modern practice (1 Samuel 28:7-14). The seer summons up Samuel, who gives Saul a message fully consistent with God's ethical concern and continuing power among the living. Modern psychics try to give grieving people evidence of the continuing life of their loved ones after the death of the body, sometimes convey important information, and encourage a confidence in God's power among both the living and the dead. Christian mediums or psychics believe that as Christ was raised from the dead, so we also can expect ourselves and our loved ones to be raised. Nevertheless, some psychics are fraudulent, and later in the chapter we will offer guidelines for those who wish to visit psychics.

Events that we would call "psychic" are honored in the New Testament and in other religious traditions as well. Here are several: the Transfiguration (Matthew 17:1-8), Jesus and the woman at the well (John 4:7-18), Paul's encounter with the risen Jesus on the road to Damascus (Acts 22:6-8), Paul's falling into a trance and hearing Jesus instruct him to leave Jerusalem (Acts 22:17-18). In

> What has been your personal view concerning psychics? What messages have you received from family and church in this regard? from personal experience? What is your impression of the popular interest in psychic work as conveyed on TV shows, movies, and books?

1 Corinthians 12:10, Paul notes that one of the spiritual gifts given to Christian people is "the ability to distinguish between spirits" (NIV).

Modern Mediums and Psychics

Early in the twentieth century, a number of leading scientists and clergy people were intensely involved in the study of mediums. They include Professor William James, scientist and spiritualist Sir Oliver Lodge, the Reverend Drayton Thomas, and many others. The great mediums, such as Mrs. Leonora Piper, Mrs. Eileen Garrett, and Mrs. Osborne Leonard, produced astonishing information that seemed to come from the deceased and worked with established research organizations, such as the American Society for Psychical Research. Most of these cautious and skeptical researchers eventually concluded that the evidence for real contact with the deceased was quite strong. On the other hand, there has been a long history of fraudulent mediums, some exposed by Houdini in the 1920's. The Committee for the Scientific Investigation of Claims of the Paranormal (CSICOP) has also been very concerned about fraud and illusion in regard to the paranormal. However, it is not likely that all or even most of the investigated reports are illusory, and professional skeptics also often have their own agendas.

In the mid-twentieth century, J. B. Rhine and his colleagues at Duke University gave strong evidence for the existence of telepathy. The logical question arose, how do we know that the details about the life of the deceased are not actually being plucked by the medium from the mind of the sitter? This developed into the "Super-ESP Hypothesis," which could then be used to challenge the most striking reports from mediums.

Here is an example. A man who lost his son went 500 miles to visit a talented psychic. The psychic said, "Your son is talking about a teddy bear. Is there a teacher or coach named Teddy Bear?" John could remember nothing related to this, thought it rather silly, and went home to his family, unimpressed with the medium. When he reported to his wife and children, they reminded him, "Don't you remember? He used to call his coach Teddy Bear."

Healthy Skepticism

In reporting this event to a skeptical friend, the friend said, "Yes, this is really striking, but how do we know that the thought of 'Teddy Bear' was not in your mind and picked up by the medium? How do we know that the medium did not read the minds of your wife and children 500 miles away?" This is an unanswerable question. The study of mediums went into decline following J. B. Rhine's research.

Form teams of three. Discuss what you would do if you were desperate for assurance that a deceased loved one is all right, but you are deeply skeptical of psychics and psychic experiences. Report back to the larger group.

But decline does not mean disappearance. Popular interest in mediums and the curiosity of researchers persisted even though skeptics mocked such interests. One of the recent students of mediumship is Gary Schwartz, Ph.D. of the University of Arizona. At some risk of ridicule and the credibility of his career, Schwartz has been doing laboratory studies of psychics for about a decade. In the preface of his 2002 book *The Afterlife Experiments,* he says, "This book is written for people who long to find scientific research that bears on what they hold most dear—that love matters, that love evolves, and that love continues forever. Discovering the existence of the living soul may be one of humankind's greatest gifts. All of this is documented here for the first time."[1]

How in the World Do You Study Psychics in a Lab?

This study is not the first time mediums have been studied in laboratory settings. But Schwartz has the advantage of knowing the huge amount of research others have done, of understanding the great difficulty of the research, and of being quite shrewd in his research design. Here is a review of a small part of Schwartz's study.[2] It is not immune from criticism and raises many questions. However, it is one important effort to bring mediumship into the laboratory, rule out some of the concerns that have plagued the field, and is a good step toward telling us more about psychic functioning.

Schwartz wanted to know whether a psychic can receive accurate readings for sitters. He also wanted to address the challenges of the scientific community that insists on double-blind studies for valid results. Without such controls, it is possible for messages to be passed, perhaps inadvertently, between sitters and psychics. Again, this is only a small piece of a large study.

An example of his research was a study of a psychic named Laurie Campbell. There were six sitters, one of whom was George Dalzell who also worked in other settings as a psychic. Laurie was not told who the sitters would be. Contact with the sitters was only by phone, with the psychic's phone muted so that there was no input from the sitters. The sitters also could not hear the psychic. (Phone contact apparently only means that a call was placed, then muted for both caller and call receiver.) The experimenters did not

> **Read on Your Own**
> Think scientifically. How do you respond to this summarized bit of research? If you were interested in mediumship and wanted to prove or disprove its validity, how would you set up a research project? What would you do differently from the way Schwartz did it?

know the order in which the various sitters would be on the phone with the psychic.

When the tapes of the psychic's six readings were transcribed, each sitter was sent two transcripts, one of his or her own reading, and one a "placebo," which belonged to another of the sitters. The transcripts did not have the names of the sitter attached, and sitters were to determine which transcript was theirs.

Only results for one of the sitters are reported in this small part of the study. Laurie Campbell's statements were 65 percent correct for George Dalzell and he was easily able to select which reading transcript was his. He believed that only 17 percent of Laurie Campbell's statements on that transcript were incorrect. Results for other psychics and other sitters are reported in other parts of Schwartz's 350 pages of material. This study is reported here to demonstrate the caution and sophistication of modern research on mediumship, which included careful isolation of mediums from sitters and a double-blind procedure. The results are striking, and other studies of Schwartz's, while too long to be reported here, are breathtaking. But they still do not rule out telepathy from the sitter to the psychic.

What About Consulting Psychics?

Because of the vulnerability of people who are in the grief process, it is often hard to make a judgment about the honesty and motivation of a psychic. For those who wish to visit psychics, here are some suggestions:

1. Read books by several psychics, such as James Van Praagh or John Edward.

2. Know how the psychic makes a living. Is the work a mission and are fees reasonable? Avoid high-priced mediums, and beware of those who ask you to return.

3. Be somewhat skeptical. Messages should be very specific. A specific message is "Your son is talking about a teacher named Teddy Bear." A suspicious question would be "Is there a man who has crossed over?" Of course! Everyone has a man who has crossed over. Be suspicious of too many questions, and give only yes or no answers. Authentic psychics will welcome questions from sitters.

> If you or someone you know has had direct experience with psychic work, or has visited a psychic, describe your experience.

4. Be aware of the selective memory phenomenon. "Your son was an extrovert" may cause you to think only of times he behaved in an extroverted manner and forget other times. Look rather for objective facts that are right or wrong.

5. Know that psychics are sometimes wrong on details, but you may expect most statements to be objectively accurate.

6. Conversation with the psychic should be after rather than before the session.

7. Ask around for referrals to good psychics, just as you would in choosing a physician.

After-Death Communications

We have discovered some of the real pitfalls in research and proof when dealing with psychics. A completely different approach has been to compile large numbers of reports of after-death communications from nonpsychics. These are usually, but not all, nonverifiable. They are often extremely convincing to the survivor. There are anthologies of reports; perhaps the largest and most recent is Bill and Judy Guggenheim's *Hello From Heaven!* The title sounds frivolous, but it is a serious account and well worth reading. It comes from a seven-year study that netted 3,300 firsthand accounts from 2,000 people from all fifty states and the ten provinces of Canada.[3] The reports are in the form reported to the Guggenheims.

A ninety-year-old writer and artist reported: "I have been contacted by my wife, Grace, many times. I have had long conversations with her. I ask her questions, and her words come into my head.

"For example, I was standing by the stove one day and felt her right beside me. I asked her, 'Do you have any advice?' And she said, 'Clean up the house now!' It was like an order. So I said, 'Okay, I will.'

"I started picking things up, and just as I got through, the doorbell rang. Three of her Delta Kappa Gamma sorority sisters came to visit me. One was the president of the whole outfit!

"I know very well that Grace knew they were coming and gave me that warning. I was amazed when this happened."[4]

A secretary reported: "Ten days after my son's death, a light appeared in my bedroom. I saw Brad's face with his eyes and his smile, and this light was around his face. I wanted to go to him and I reached out with my arms.

"Brad said, 'Mom, I'm all right.' I knew what he was saying because it was like it went directly into my head. I said, 'Son, I want to be with you.' He shook his head and smiled, saying, 'No, it's not your time, Mom.' He had a look of peace and happiness as he went away.

"Then I rolled over with a feeling of peace and had the best sleep since Brad had died."[5]

A seventy-year-old retired nurse reported that Graham, her brother-in-law, gave her a message after his death. "Graham passed away when he was eighty-nine years old. I guess his heart just gave out. I had this experience with him before I knew he had died.

"I felt his presence in my kitchen. He said to me, 'Tell Vera,' who is my sister, 'to look real good around the desk in her living room. Take the drawers out and look in the back.'

"I wrote a letter to Vera and explained my experience to her. Then later my niece called me. She told me they went through the desk and found about $3,000 in $50 bills he had hidden away!

"Obviously, Graham wanted Vera to find the money so it wouldn't be thrown out accidentally. All through his life his main interest seemed to be money, but I think he was more concerned about his wife's security."[6]

> If you have felt a mystical connection to nature or to an animal or another person, please describe that experience. What about the experience causes you to think of it as nonordinary? What connections do you see, if any, between such experiences and after-death communication? What position, if any, would you think your church could take regarding attempts to communicate with deceased loved ones?

The Guggenheims estimate that 50,000,000 people in the U.S. have had such experiences, and say that ADCs are also very common in other parts of the world, where they are taken as real communications from the deceased.[7] This writer believes that in our culture almost no one reports such experiences unless directly asked, for fear of ridicule. Even medical doctors and pastors almost never hear of such reports. Yet there is profound joy, trust, and new life associated with these events; and if we recall the findings on NDEs, DBVs, OBE, and apparitions, we may conclude that not only are they profoundly meaningful, but some are likely to be "objectively" real as well.

Communion of the Saints

"I believe in the Holy Spirit, the holy catholic church, the communion of saints, the forgiveness of sins, the resurrection of the body, and the life everlasting." These familiar words from the Apostles' Creed are used in most Protestant churches. The words linger; but they are, unfortunately for Protestants, rather like the bones of a once-robust but long-vanished assurance of our connection with those who have gone before us in faith. The phrase, "communion of saints" was first used in the Eastern churches, then in the Apostles' Creed formulated by the Roman Church at the end of the fifth century. It gradually came to imply the communion between the earthly church and the heavenly church, between those who have passed on and those who remain in earthly life. Saints came to be seen not only as

> What traditions have you seen in your family and your church family concerning communicating with the saints? about communicating with deceased loved ones? What impact, if any, have the reference to the communion of saints in the Apostles' Creed and in the preface to the canon of the Eucharist had for you? Where would you stand on the issue of invoking the saints to pray to God on your behalf, versus praying to the saints? What are the reasons for your belief?

those believers faithful to God here on earth but also those in heaven. The union of spiritual wayfarers in the life on earth is in no way interrupted when some pass on.

Vatican II, which closed in 1965, placed great emphasis on the communion that exists between the faithful on earth and the blessed in heaven and urged that this doctrine be developed and explained. The communion of saints is seen as a continuum between the church in pilgrimage and the church in its destiny. So the practice of invoking the saints, when done according to Roman Catholic doctrine, does not involve praying to the saints, but rather asking the saints to pray to God on our behalf. Protestants have emphasized this as well. It is similar to our asking a friend to pray for us; we do not pray to the friend, but ask the friend to pray to God. If my friend should die, and I believe in a continuing life after the death

> Read or sing the hymns "For All the Saints," "I Sing a Song of the Saints of God," and "Ye Watchers and Ye Holy Ones." What connections do you make between the words to these hymns and after-death communication?

of the body, then logically I should be able to ask my friend to pray to God on my behalf.

A French Protestant, R. Paquier, encourages Protestants to honor the saints: "It is right that the Church should put aside a day in order to bring to mind 'the great cloud of witnesses' by whom we are surrounded (Hebr. 12. 1), and to thank the Lord for having raised up so many older brothers and sisters whose example moves and encourages us. They are not dead, but alive in God (Luke 20. 38...); they are the living crown of Christ the King."[8]

Encounters With the Risen Christ

In Chapter 4, we examined the post-Resurrection appearances of Jesus as reported in the New Testament. But are there not more recent encounters with the risen Christ? Christian history is filled with such accounts, in the lives of the saints, in the experiences of church founders such as Joseph Smith and George Fox, in the reported appearances at Catholic shrines, and even to individuals, such as Kim Dae Jung, a political leader in South Korea. There are a number of collections, one by G. Scott Sparrow, of cases in which there is no near-death experience or deathbed vision, but rather events more like the apparitional events discussed in Chapter 4. Here are two examples.

"I dreamed I was standing atop a mountain. I looked skyward and saw a bright golden light. As I stared at it, it turned into the most brilliant white light I have ever seen. In the center of the light I saw the face of Christ appear. After gazing at his face I saw what looked like comets shooting this way and that. One landed close to where I was standing and burst into flames.

"I awoke and it felt like I was coming out of anesthesia. There is no question in my mind whether or not it was Jesus. You just know. He is the guiding and/or controlling force in my life."[9]

"Then he came to me in an appearance that was sudden, intense and brief. I was in one of my depressions—one of my crying jags when I felt totally worthless and unloved, self-hating, and alone. In my black pit there was suddenly a window thrown open and love and light streamed down on me. I saw the Christ and he said to me, 'You are loved.' It was there for one clear instant and then it was gone and I was reeling from it. The depth of my being felt changed and I have since felt an inner confidence in the love that is there and in the certainty of Christ's reality."[10]

Is There a Place for Such Encounters in the Life of the Church?

We would think the answer to this question should be obvious. These are reports of experiences we might call "mystical." They remind us of NDE and DBV accounts and of the post-Resurrection appearances of Jesus in the New Testament. Yet, it is not easy to find any sign in the doctrines, or even the practices, of many Protestant churches that such direct experiences are to be honored or trusted. The language in the doctrines is general, with references to the Holy Spirit and to salvation but not to encounters with the risen Lord. And there is widespread discomfort about the "enthusiasm" or emotionality involved in these direct experiences. Yet, many people wish for these experiences. Some hymns of the churches also express a desire for these encounters, for example, "Into My Heart," "Love Divine, All Loves Excelling," "Have Thine Own Way, Lord," and "Come, Thou Almighty King."

> Find the hymns mentioned in this section (or other hymns about the risen Christ) in your church's hymnal. Sing or read the words. What, if anything do they say to you about experiences of the risen Christ?

An Encouraging Summary

Some church leaders argue strongly that we have been too intellectual, perhaps impersonal, in our approach to religious experience. They feel that the depth and emotionality of direct encounters with Christ should not be pushed to the fringe of Christian life. In fact, many church people report such events, but say they have not shared them for fear of ridicule, even in the church. Such encounters do fit with the findings of our research. It seems reasonable that if we can communicate with those who have predeceased us, we should be able to communicate with the risen Christ, according to his promise. If he is risen as we believe, then that risen Christ

> What practices do you see in the church that do or could enhance the likelihood of personal encounters with the risen Christ? What things would you like to see develop on the basis of the things you have studied in this chapter?

is just as available to modern people as he was to the early believers in the post-Resurrection appearances. There are signs of spiritual renewal, with an encouragement and a facilitating of these kinds of experiences. If these encounters are honored in the context of worship, Scripture, experience, and tradition, they give the clearest possible basis for a Christ-centered and resurrected life. They also offer to each person a full confidence in a continuing resurrection after the death of the body.

Closing
   Consider the complexity of assessing after-death communications, and give thanks for the continuing efforts researchers are making to explore this difficult area. Ask for guidance in your own spiritual development. Also ask for wisdom to sort out the wheat from the chaff in this area and so grow into a genuine New Testament faith in the resurrection of Jesus and in our own resurrections.

Notes

1. From *The Afterlife Experiments,* by Gary Schwartz, (Pocket Books, New York, 2002); page XVI.

2. From *The Afterlife Experiments,* pages 235–36.

3. From *Hello From Heaven!* by Bill and Judy Guggenheim (Bantam Books, New York, 1997); page 19.

4. From *Hello From Heaven!;* page 46.

5. From *Hello From Heaven!;* page 79.

6. From *Hello From Heaven!;* page 282.

7. From *Hello From Heaven!;* page 21.

8. From *The Communion of Saints,* by Emilien Lamirande (Hawthorn Books: New York, 1963); page 152.

9. From *I Am With You Always,* by G. Scott Sparrow (Bantam, New York, 1995); page 40.

10. From *I Am With You Always;* pages 78–79.

For More Information
Internet Links—Use the following Internet addresses for additional information:

http://survivalafterdeath.org/reviews/schwartz01.htm
http://journeysproject.com/links.asp
http://www.xs4all.nl/~wichm/paraps.html

CHAPTER 7
LIVING IN THE PROMISE
OF ETERNAL LIFE

"But Christ has indeed been rised from the dead, the first fruits of those who have fallen asleep. For since death came through a man, the resurrection of the dead comes also through a man. For as in Adam all die, so in Christ will all be made alive."

—1 Corinthians 15:20-22, NIV

Focus

This chapter explores practical ways individuals and groups can live in the hope and promise of life beyond death.

An Announcement of Very Good News

Hope for a life after the death of the physical body may well be the most vital of all human issues. Most world religions have in their own way addressed the issue and concluded that there are powerful reasons for being confident about a spiritual life beyond the physical body. The New Testament is uncompromising in its certainty of resurrection, both for Jesus and for the ordinary person of faith. And there is modern research that supports such certainty. Yet, the omnipresent materialistic focus in our culture has eroded this age-old confidence. Even many modern theologians avoid dealing directly with resurrection. Pastors, having studied the works of the theologians in divinity school, sometimes are not themselves confident about resurrection. Understandably, some have trouble counseling people with questions about eternal life and questions of bereaved people about the well-being of loved ones who have died. Added

Gathering

Greet one another. Tell about one thing that impressed you or challenged you in the previous sessions. Offer a prayer of gratitude for the resurrection of Jesus and the Resurrection life that you can live. Ask for God's guidance as you seek ways in which the Spirit may be calling for you or the group to share faith in life beyond death.

to this, many of us avoid even thinking about death until we are forced to do so; and death, because we are so unprepared for it, becomes even more a tragedy than it needs to be.

This study has been an attempt to respond to these problems. Many fortunate people have the gift of an unfailing confidence about resurrection that is not based on study and research. In a society that is so influenced by science and so materially oriented, however, many people lack this certainty. They may believe that such faith is naive or unrealistic. Most people do not know that serious research has been done on life after death, and that the research strongly supports a New Testament faith. Churches have an opportunity to nurture confidence in people about the meaning of their lives and the fate of their loved ones. They can provide opportunities to explore Scriptures, research, and questions about life beyond death, and thus strengthen the message of the church, based as it is, historically, on the Resurrection. When we understand and believe the Resurrection, then preaching, biblical and theological study, the sacraments, prayer, mission, and especially evangelism take on a new excitement and a new urgency.

In the previous chapters we looked at the research and New Testament teachings in the areas of near-death experiences (NDEs), deathbed visions (DBVs), out-of-body experiences (OBEs), apparitions, reincarnation, and after-death communication (ADC). We have learned, especially from NDEs and DBVs, that people who are close to death seem to receive a glimpse of another reality. The experiences are cross-cultural, are similar for large numbers of people, and do not usually seem related to drugs or physical or mental conditions or even belief or disbelief in such experiences or their reality. Those who have such experiences often encounter entities that they believe are deceased loved ones, religious figures, or otherworldly landscapes. They report these encounters and sometimes are greatly surprised at the visions they see. A certainty about life after death usually accompanies the experiences. Those who are skeptical of the truth of such experiences need to discount the implications of many of the facts that have emerged. The long-term effects of the NDE, on those who hear of it as well as on those who experience it, are profound and permanent. Interpretations of NDEs and DBVs range from mechanistic views that the experiences are results of chemical changes in the brain to spiritual views that the experiences are channels through which God speaks to us.

81

In what ways does Christian faith say something similar to the variety of experiences presented in this study? In what ways does Christian faith say something different? What remains open to speculation?

Out-of-body experiences and apparitions, while not as widely discussed as NDEs, may provide yet stronger evidence of life after death. Some OBEs, in which other people see the apparitional form of the OBE projector are well-researched and quite convincing. And the OBE certainly suggests that there is a "nonphysical"component that can function outside of, and perhaps independently of, the physical body. Skeptical views are that OBEs are drug reactions or dreams, and each person may choose which interpretation fits best. Apparitions have received considerable critical research, but there has been less public discussion. Cases in which apparitions give information that is previously unknown but proves to be accurate are difficult to explain away. Further, apparitions sometimes behave in ways that seem best explained in "physical" terms, but at other times in ways best explained in "nonphysical" or "spiritual" terms. There are OBE reports in both the Hebrew Scriptures and the New Testament. Many view OBEs and apparitions as support for New Testament claims of the resurrection of Jesus and the resurrection we may anticipate for ourselves and our loved ones.

Reincarnation ideas provide an especially interesting topic of discussion. We have seen that there is some persuasive evidence supporting some form of rebirth, but for some Christians reincarnation thinking suggests a strong challenge to Christian theology. For others, reincarnation helps to explain some strange events and is easily incorporated in their Christian faith. After-death communication has emerged as a popular topic since Bill and Judy Guggenheim made a large collection of modern reports from all fifty states and all the provinces of Canada and reported them in *Hello From Heaven!* (see Chapter 6). Though unresearched, some are quite convincing and form another part of the tapestry that includes the other topics we have discussed.

Altogether, the six areas provide fascinating, and for many, convincing evidence of life after death. And they provide support for a Christian faith in the resurrection of Jesus and in resurrection for our loved ones and ourselves.

Now we turn to practical ways that Christian people and their churches can live a Resurrection life.

Resurrection and Bereavement

People who have lost a loved one to death, or who are facing death themselves, are facing one of the deepest crises of their lives. For many people, good pastoral counseling is helpful in working through the crisis. But Christian people have an additional resource that, even in the churches, is underused. We have learned from experience and from research on the NDE that many bereaved people, and many who are not bereaved, will have a life-changing response to this relatively new information. When they learn that modern research on life after death and the New Testament witness about life after death fit neatly together, there can be a deep renewal of faith, a rise in confidence, and progress in the resolution of the most painful grief. Resurrection becomes vivid, and every day is Easter.

What is your personal experience with grief? How has your Christian faith related to your experience of grief? Please describe any experience you have had or have observed of grief being transformed into a deepened Resurrection faith.

Neal Grossman lists the results from research that are being reconfirmed almost daily: there is an afterlife, our real identity is not our body, but our mind or consciousness; the purpose of life is love and knowledge—to learn as much as possible about this world and the transcendent world, to grow in our ability to feel kindness and compassion toward all beings, and to learn that a consequence of the life review is that it appears to be a great disadvantage to oneself to harm another person, since the pain one inflicts on another is experienced as one's own in the life review.[1]

If this new learning based upon scientific methods of research on the variety of experiences we have explored in this book were seriously considered in the seminaries, in pastoral counseling education, and in local churches, Paul's words, "Death has been swallowed up in victory," could be understood in a new and deeper way. Moreover, if we became, on the basis of this new learning, more than ever convinced of Christ's resurrection, direct encounters with Christ would become more likely for us. When the continuing life of our loved ones becomes a confidence based on reason as well as faith, we become more able to receive after-death communications from them. And we find ourselves facing our own death, and life, with a new faith, a new peace, and even with exuberance, which is the essence of meaning in living a Christian Resurrection life.

83

> Do you think it is helpful to legitimize the after-death phenomena as in this paragraph? Or do you think such legitimization opens a door for abuses, confusion, and wishful thinking? Explain your response.

Bereaved people could benefit from affirmations of experiences like sensing the presence of the deceased, hearing a voice of the deceased, feeling a touch from the deceased, seeing an appearance, having vivid dreams of the deceased, experiencing unusual natural phenomena apparently related to the deceased, or seeing mechanical or electrical gadgets behave strangely. In fact, research and experience show that such events may well be after-death communications.

Confirmation of the Spiritual Values

Neal Grossman also points out that the religions of the world largely agree that divine love is the force that creates and sustains our world. Acknowledging divine love involves practicing compassion and forgiveness. Divine love requires that we treat people as unique and valued simply because they exist and that we do not inordinately value material possessions. Divine love helps us anticipate and inform others about a life after death. NDEers confirm all of these values. According to Grossman,

> Knowing that there are central values common to the world religions, how would you feel most comfortable in describing the unique aspects of your Christian faith with a group including adherents of other faiths?

as long as these values are presented merely as religious values, it is easy for anyone to give them lip service, especially on Sunday mornings. But when these values are presented as confirmed, scientific hypotheses rising from careful research on the NDE, they become more difficult to ignore.[2] Further research on NDEs and other kinds of experiences will encourage such values. Perhaps we may anticipate a "sea change" in the way people think about such issues, as the research findings become more widely known.

Christians may, with even more confidence than before, encourage and profess these values. We can also learn how they emerge in other faiths, from adherents to those faiths, and point out to those interested that there is a research as well as a faith foundation for the teachings of the New Testament.

Mysticism and Nonordinary States of Consciousness

Many people who study the material on life after death do so because they have personally had unusual experiences that have inspired, puzzled or frightened them. These include pre-cognitive dreams, after-death communications, reincarnation memories, encounters with deceased loved ones, or encounters with God or with the risen Christ. Findings in life-after-death studies show that these experiences are part of a broad spectrum of nonordinary human experiences and can have a most profound positive impact our lives. They have parallels in the Bible, as well as in the Scriptures of the world religions. They are to be coveted and honored, rather than feared. But more than this, overemphasis on a rational and sometimes intellectual approach to faith, and not enough emphasis on enabling people to have profound mystical or spiritual experiences, limits the way persons can understand and experience religious knowledge. Churches have an opportunity to acquaint people not only with the vast literature on life-after-death experiences but also on the varieties of religious experience and especially to inform them about Christian mystics and mystics in other religious traditions. Such nonordinary experiences, especially encounters with the risen Christ, should be affirmed as a part of a rich tradition in Christian faith. There is a place in the Christian life and in the churches for careful and thoughtful intel-

> Describe any unusual, paranormal, or spiritual experience that you or someone you know has had. Over time, what has been the impact of the experience on your life?

> Visit *www.textweek.com/art/ resurrection_of_Christ.htm*. Print out some of the fine art pictures of the Resurrection. Which pictures do you find most speak to you? Why?

> Consider as a group whether there is currently enough encouragement and help for people who would like to open themselves to mystical or visionary experiences. What could be done or where could a person go in your area to enhance this aspect of spirituality?

lectual study and also for deeply emotional, even visionary and paranormal experiences.

An Opportunity for Evangelism

Many opportunities exist for local churches to educate people about the research and biblical ideas regarding life after death. In additon, considerable interest exists outside the churches in life after death and in parapsychological research. Even organizations of skeptics have recently recognized that much parapsychological research is of the very highest standard. For people on a spiritual path, who are asking profound questions about meaning and about life after death, study of life-after-death issues provides a meeting point between the parapsychological discoveries and Christian faith. This is an opportunity for evangelism of a special kind, sharply focused for people who have already embarked on their own spiritual search. People need to hear about the research, to hear that one form of new life is resurrection, and to hear that we share in this promise. In this way they will see that Christian faith can illuminate the path in which they already have great interest. This approach reminds us of the way Paul articulated Christian faith so that Greek people could understand and appreciate it, by using some of their ideas, words, and thought categories. (See Acts 17:15-32.)

Read Acts 17:15-32. If your pastor is not a regular member of your group, invite him or her to describe the way Paul used Greek ideas and language to convey Christian faith to Greek people. Explore how this might relate to sophisticated efforts at evangelism to modern people. Contemporary music and contemporary worship services are familiar examples. What else could be done? Is it realistic to approach evangelism through education about life after death?

One hundred years ago, William James pointed out that when scientific-rational thinking and deep personal experience unite, there is born a powerful religious faith. This is as true now as then and can inform our efforts at evangelism.

The Search for Meaning

Many people, perhaps the most thoughtful and educated among us, experience what may be called a "crisis of meaning." Sometimes the loss of a loved one, or a job, or a marriage, leads to an adolescent, young adult, middle age, or other crisis that goes beyond the grief over what has been lost and moves to a sense of the loss of life's meaning. This can also result from an academic study of philosophies of nothing-ness (nihilism), meaninglessness, atheistic existentialism, or even materialist science. Some people seriously ask, "What is the point of all this effort?" or "Is it possible really to know anything?" At root this is a spiritual question as well as a philosophical and practical one. Experience shows that evidence that there is a life after death can help such thoughtful people place their experience in a completely different context. How can life be meaningless if there is more to life than the physical body? How can the loss in death of a loved one be the end of the story? If the research findings and the New Testament are true, does this not suggest that love, forgiveness, compassion, and a continuing spiritual life are at the heart of reality, rather than nausea, suffering, and meaninglessness?

> How important, in your experience, is the search for meaning? Where have you gone for answers to your questions of meaning? What does Christian faith say about life's meaning? What do you think of the idea that every individual's life has a special meaning or purpose and that a most important role of church and family is to help the individual in discovering it?

Therapy for Death Anxiety

Considerable research suggests that the fear of death is largely repressed, or put out of mind, but that unconscious anxiety about death fuels the more obvious anxieties. The universal (and commercially profitable) interest and admiration people have for heroes facing death may well rise from our own fear. The challenges heroes face remind us of our own struggles and the ultimate challenge of death. We admire the

> How do you feel about the claim that repressed death anxiety is an important issue for most people? How does our culture as a whole deal with death? Who are your personal heroes or heroines? What do you most admire, and why? What, if any, connection does your admiration have to your feelings about death?

87

hero who faces and conquers fear and death. General fear, anxiety disorders, phobias, compulsions have all been linked to a deeper death anxiety. Lifestyle issues of materialistic striving, compulsive behaviors, and substance abuse may be linked as well. And even though many people say they believe in life after death, when death occurs, it is usually seen as an unmitigated tragedy. This suggests that confidence in a continuing life, and in resurrection, is for many people, even Christians, rather superficial.

Because thoughts about death are so avoided and yet so significant a part of the human predicament, the message of resurrection, if made believable, amounts to the deepest kind of psycho-spiritual therapy. This may explain the documented, life-changing impact of NDEs and of learning about the connection between life-after-death research and Christian ideas about resurrection. One reason for the rapid spread of Christianity in the early centuries of the church was that the focus on Christ's resurrection gave a new hope to early believers about their own survival of death. Such hope offered triumph over despair. There is no reason why the churches cannot offer the same hope in modern times to modern people.

A New Tool for Moral Education

All thinking people recognize the importance of moral education, especially in the schools and churches as well as in the family. It is not wishful thinking to imagine that with better worldwide moral education, the mass murders of the twentieth century and the continuing bloodshed in this century, the recent corporate scandals, as well as many of the daily moral tragedies we experience, could have been prevented. We need every tool we can imagine to influence the personal, political, and economic forces that control our lives and culture. One important area of education consists of moral education, and an Internet search will show the very large amount of research and teaching that is already occurring, even outside the churches and family.

Profound life changes that come for those who experience life-after-death events, and even for those who only hear about them, have implications for moral education. For centuries, the "Hearing of the Gospel" has produced profound changes in people's lives. The focus in many of these modern life-after-death experiences on love, on

> What about life-after-death studies might make this a vital issue in moral education?

relationships, on forgiveness and responsibility, apparently happens in such a way that the impact on one's daily life actions and choices is often immediate and profound. The life review also touches on the issue of judgment. All of this suggests that it would be useful if education about the NDE and other life-after-death issues could happen in public and private schools, in families, and especially in Christian education, both for children and adults. John C. Gibbs, consulting editor for the *Journal of Near-Death Studies,* has already done research on the NDE in moral education. We believe the research on life after death is an important tool that we cannot afford to leave unused.

The Role of Churches

Churches traditionally do an excellent job with attending to bereavement by providing meals, support, cards, prayers, pastoral care, funeral services that celebrate life. As suggested above, such beneficial care of the bereaved can be enriched with a variety of ministries that might emerge from topics related to research on reports of the variety of experiences of life beyond death. These could include, perhaps even on an interchurch basis, small groups that study and anticipate the process of bereavement, support groups that specifically allow or encourage discussion of paranormal experiences. Experience shows that very many people have a strong need to share such nonordinary experiences, but have felt reluctant because they feared ridicule, or misunderstanding.

> List some creative ministries that your local church or area churches could initiate in addition to the traditional ones related to bereavement.

Full Circle

We have seen that scientific exploration strongly supports the claim of the New Testament writers about Jesus' resurrection and the promise of our own. Great thinkers, from Jesus and Paul to William James and modern researchers on life after death, teach us in a variety of ways that reasonable arguments plus spiritual experience equals power. So Paul wrote, in a way that seemed very reasonable to the Corinthians, "Since death came through a human being, the resurrection of the dead has also come through a human being; for as all die in Adam, so all will be made alive in Christ" (1 Corinthians 15:21-22). Resurrection faith is indeed powerful.

Closing

Sing the hymn, "Be Thou My Vision." Read Numbers 12:6. Consider the impact this study has had on you. Consider how this material might be made available for those who need it in your community. Give thanks for the powerful evidence that supports the Christian claim and promise of resurrection. Ask for illumination at the deepest level, and commit yourself to conscious living of a resurrected life.

Notes

1. From "Who's Afraid of Life After Death?" by Neal Grossman. *Journal of Near Death Studies,* Vol. 21, Number 1, Fall 2002; pages 21–22.

2. From "Who's Afraid of Life After Death?" pages 20–21.

For More Information

Internet Key Words—Type the following words and phrases into an Internet search program for additional information:

Christian Art Resurrection
Moral Education
Death Anxiety
Christian Existentialism

Internet Links—Use the following Internet addresses for additional information:

http://human-nature.com/reason/james/contents.html
www.meaning.ca/articles/death_acceptance.htm

BIBLIOGRAPHY

Barrett, William. *Death Bed Visions: The Physical Experiences of the Dying (Colin Wilson Library of the Paranormal)*. New York: HarperCollins, 1988.

Blackmore, Susan. *Beyond the Body*. Chicago: Academy Chicago Publishers, 1982.

Bowman, Carol. *Children's Past Lives: How Past Life Memories Affect Your Child*. New York: Bantam, 1998.

Currie, Ian. *You Cannot Die*. Toronto: Somerville House, 1998.

Greenhouse, Herbert. *The Astral Journey*. New York: Doubleday and Company, 1975.

Moody, Jr., Raymond A. *Life After Life*. New York. Bantam Books, 1982.

_____. *The Light Beyond*. New York: Bantam Books, 1989.

Morse, Melvin. *Closer to the Light: Learning from the Near-Death Experiences of Children*. New York: Ivy Books, 1991.

_____. *Where God Lives: The Science of the Paranormal and How Our Brains Are Linked to the Universe*. Cliff Street Books, 2000.

_____. *Transformed by the Light: The Powerful Effect of Near Death Experiences on People's Lives*. Villard Books, 1992.

Osis, Karlis and Haraldsson, Erlendur. *At the Hour of Death*. New York: TimeLife, 1993.

Ring, Kenneth. *Life at Death*. William Morrow & Company, 1982.

_____. *Heading Toward Omega*. William Morrow & Company, 1984.

_____. *Lessons from the Light: What We Can Learn from the Near-Death Experience*. Portsmouth, New Hampshire: Moment Point Press, 2000.

Sabom, Michael B. *Light and Death: One Doctor's Fascinating Account of Near-Death Experiences*. Grand Rapids, Michigan: Zondervan, 1998.

Wills-Brandon, Carla. *One Last Hug Before I Go: The Mystery and Meaning of Deathbed Visions*. Health Communications, 2000.